IAN CARTER

BOMBER COMMAND 1939-45

PHOTOGRAPHS FROM THE IMPERIAL WAR MUSEUM

Ian Allan
PUBLISHING

CONTENTS

Above:
Bostons of No 2 Group over the target during the daylight raid on the Philips radio and valve factories at Eindhoven, 6 December 1942. Operation 'Oyster' involved 93 aircraft — Bostons, Venturas and Mosquitos — but the target was well beyond the range of available fighter cover. Various diversionary raids took place, including an attack by American B-17s on Lille, but these did not prevent heavy losses, with 14 aircraft being shot down. Despite the losses, this most ambitious of all No 2 Group's raids was a strategic success, inflicting serious damage on a vitally important target. **C 5755**

Title page:
Wellingtons of No 300 (Masovian) Squadron at Hemswell, 17 June 1943. All aircraft bear the Polish Air Force national insignia below the cockpit. The foreground aircraft also sports 'nose art' in the shape of 'Grumpy', one of Walt Disney's 'Seven Dwarves'. The squadron was next in action on the night of 21/22 June, when Bomber Command attacked Krefeld in the Ruhr. Two aircraft from the squadron failed to return, and another crashed during an air test before the raid. All fifteen aircrew involved were killed. **CH 10456**

First published 2000

ISBN 0 7110 2699 8

© Ian Carter 2000

Published by Ian Allan Publishing

an imprint of Ian Allan Publishing Ltd, Terminal House, Shepperton, Surrey TW17 8AS.
Printed by Ian Allan Printing Ltd, Riverdene Business Park, Hersham, Surrey KT12 4RG.

Code: 0002/c

PREFACE

This book presents a photographic portrait of Royal Air Force Bomber Command's offensive against Germany during World War 2. It was a protracted and costly campaign, which, after a hesitant start, gradually evolved into a major, if not decisive, contribution to the defeat of Hitler. Tactics became more sophisticated and effective; aircraft and equipment underwent constant and rapid development; an organisational structure of huge complexity evolved to support a bomber force whose size and power grew inexorably. The cost to both sides was enormous; the results clouded by controversy. I do not seek to enter the moral or strategic debate; many fuller and more penetrating studies cover this ground. However, the courage and sacrifice of the aircrews, and the dedication of so many more who built, serviced, trained or otherwise served, is incontrovertible, and is the principal theme of this work.

All the images have been selected from the Imperial War Museum's Photograph Archive. The vast majority come from the Air Ministry official series, taken by members of the RAF Film & Photographic Unit, or by commercial photographers, and released through the Ministry of Information. The rest are from the Archive's holdings of American, Australian and Canadian official photographs, and from a handful of the many collections generously donated to the Museum or lent for copying by private individuals over the years. While the extensive Ministry holdings provide a rich source, those photographs which were snapped privately (invariably against regulations!) help fill some of the many gaps in the official coverage. There are doubtless many other gems in the attics of veterans or their families, still awaiting discovery.

The selection has to a considerable extent been dictated by the available material. Photographs taken on actual operations were few and far between, and many events went virtually unrecorded. The 'front-line' of the bomber offensive was the cramped, darkened (and secret) confines of an aircraft over enemy territory; this precluded any kind of visual record. Instead, the attention of official photographers was usually focused on the airfields from which the squadrons operated,

enabling the multiplicity of tasks performed by the ground personnel to be portrayed. For obvious reasons, the authorities chose not to communicate the horrific reality of operations, but there is poignancy even in those photographs that were released; witness the nervous smiles on the faces of crews about to set off on a raid, perhaps never to return, or the strain visible on those crowded wearily around tables during debriefing afterwards. German photographs of the shattered remains of downed aircraft bear testimony to the terrible losses; 55,500 aircrew (out of 125,000) died in Bomber Command's war, and it is worth remembering that many of the young men whose faces are glimpsed in this book were destined to be among them.

In view of their sacrifice, it seems only right that the operations of the Advanced Air Striking Force in France during 1939/40 — No 1 Group in all but name — and those of the No 2 Group Blenheim squadrons which operated with the Air Component of the British Expeditionary Force, should be granted inclusion in this book, even if the units concerned were technically outside Bomber Command control for much of the time. No 2 Group itself eventually left Bomber Command in June 1943, but its dramatic early daylight operations made for some arresting images. Because this book is about the offensive role of Bomber Command, I have not covered the work of the two Special Duties squadrons within No 3 Group, Nos 161 and 138, which spent most of the war ferrying agents and supplies to resistance groups in Europe. Unsurprisingly, their activities were not revealed to official photographers. In contrast, I would like to have included more on another secretive and little-photographed organisation, No 100 (Bomber Support) Group. Many other units within Bomber Command were not officially photographed at all, which might seem surprising, but as the war progressed there was so much more to record, and the bomber offensive gradually lost much of its novelty value. At least the return to daylight bombing by the Main Force in the summer of 1944 enabled some dramatic images to be inadvertently captured by the strike cameras aboard the aircraft themselves.

The captions are based initially on the information contained in wartime Air Ministry files, currently located in the Photograph Archive. Official captions were, of course, subject to the normal rules of wartime censorship and therefore the identities of locations and units were often withheld, but useful information was sometimes recorded for internal purposes. In addition, I have referred to a host of published sources, two of which deserve special mention right at the beginning. *The Bomber Command War Diaries* by Martin Middlebrook and Chris Everitt is the definitive reference book on Bomber Command operations and is quite simply indispensable. W. R. Chorley's mammoth six-volume work of research *RAF Bomber Command Losses of the Second World War* is both incredibly useful and immeasurably sad. Even the most cursory examination of these volumes, each with its memorial-like listings of missing crews, cannot fail to move the reader; I can think of no more vivid a testament to the vast sacrifice of the men of Bomber Command. I gratefully acknowledge the use I have made of this research, and that of the many other authors whose excellent books are listed in the bibliography.

I would like to acknowledge the assistance of the Keeper and my colleagues in the Imperial War Museum Photograph Archive, especially Richard Bayford, Paul Coleman and Gordon McLeod in the darkrooms. Permission to reproduce material from the Official History (*The Strategic Air Offensive against* *Germany, 1939-1945* by Sir Charles Webster and Noble Frankland) was kindly supplied by the Controller of Her Majesty's Stationery Office. I also wish to thank Crécy Publishing for permission to use an extract from Guy Gibson's *Enemy Coast Ahead* (© 1946 Royal Air Force Museum) and Greenhill Books for allowing me to quote from *Bomber Offensive* by Sir Arthur Harris. Thanks too go to Roger Freeman and Jerry Scutts for taking the trouble to help me with the odd query when they were trying to carry out their own research. Above all, I would like to thank my parents and especially my wife, Marian, for their practical and moral support, without which this book would never have got off the ground.

Left:
Four years before the outbreak of World War 2, the Royal Air Force had 14 home-based bomber squadrons: eight were equipped with Fairey Gordon and Hawker Hart light bombers, five with Handley Page Heyford and Vickers Virginia heavy bombers, and a solitary medium bomber squadron, No 101, was operating the Boulton Paul Overstrand. All were biplane designs, and all were between five and twelve years old! The Overstrand, which first equipped No 101 Squadron in January 1935, was a popular aircraft with its crews, and featured the RAF's first power-operated gun turret, but was incapable of reaching targets in continental Europe. It remained in service as a short-term expedient, pending the arrival of modern monoplane bombers. This photograph shows Overstrands at King George V's Jubilee Review at RAF Mildenhall, Suffolk, in July 1935. In June 1938 No 101 Squadron began re-equipping with Blenheims. **HU 3658**

Right:
Last of the RAF's biplane bombers, the Handley Page Heyford first entered service with No 99 Squadron at Upper Heyford, Oxfordshire, in November 1933. It had originally been ordered as a stop-gap before the arrival of the more advanced Fairey Hendon monoplane bomber, but problems with that aircraft meant that Heyford production was stepped up; by the end of 1936 — the year in which Bomber Command was created — nine squadrons were equipped with the type. This aircraft, a Mk III, was on strength with No 102 Squadron at Honington in Suffolk. The Heyford remained the mainstay of Bomber Command's heavy bomber force for five years, and was finally superseded by the new Wellington and Whitley bombers in 1938. **HU 58005**

INTRODUCTION

'[Bomber Command is]...entirely unprepared for war, unable to operate except in fair weather and extremely vulnerable both in the air and on the ground.'

(Air Chief Marshal Sir Edgar Ludlow-Hewitt, Air Officer Commanding-in-Chief, Bomber Command, November 1937)

The outbreak of World War 2 in September 1939 found Royal Air Force Bomber Command neither properly equipped, nor sufficiently trained, to carry out the role for which it had been intended. Its shortcomings, the true extent of which had yet to be fully revealed and were by no means unique to the RAF, were the result of half a decade of hasty and uneven expansion, following years of stagnation and snail-like technical development. In the two decades after the end of the Great War, the RAF established its own independent role through the evolution of a bombing doctrine that espoused the primacy of the bomber as a decisive weapon of war; a doctrine that would profoundly influence the course of RAF strategy in the coming conflict. No other combatant nation had prepared to carry out a strategic bombing offensive, but in Britain, as war with Germany approached, detailed operational plans for such a campaign were formulated. Moreover, despite the inadequacies of prewar rearmament programmes, vitally important production policy decisions were taken. Thus, although Bomber Command went to war only half ready, with barely adequate aircraft and deficient in most areas of training and equipment, the foundations had been laid for a bombing force of unrivalled strength and effectiveness, which would carry the war to Germany and contribute massively to the eventual Allied victory.

The latter half of the 1930s saw a massive increase in the numerical strength of the Royal Air Force, and the advent of a range of new bomber designs, as Britain hastily rearmed to face the threat from Hitler and Nazi Germany. Such urgency was necessary due to the effects of the period of disarmament and political naivety that had gone before. Although Britain had emerged from World War 1 with the most powerful air force in the world, this new independent service had been allowed to dwindle to a shadow of itself during the following decade. Financial stringency, exacerbated by economic depression, and the unwillingness of a population repelled by the events of 1914-18 even to consider the possibility of another war, meant that armaments came far down the list of priorities of the Government of the day. That the Royal Air Force even survived as an independent arm was due to the efforts of its foremost champion, Sir Hugh Trenchard, who had commanded the Royal Flying Corps in France, and who held the post of Chief of the

Air Staff from 1919 to 1929. Under him, the infant service was nurtured and its basic organisation and structure established. Trenchard believed wholeheartedly in the power of aerial bombing, maintaining that the prime function of the aeroplane was as a weapon of offence. In 1918 he had commanded the 'Independent Force', formed to carry out strategic night attacks on Germany, whose airships and Gotha bombers had already been bombing Britain. Trenchard believed that the effects of bombing on the morale of the civilian population would greatly exceed any material damage that might be inflicted; a conflict could be won by air power alone, without the intervention of armies. The war ended before his theory, which would have a profound influence on the future of Bomber Command, could be put to the test.

In the 1920s, the Royal Air Force was kept alive by its usefulness in quelling unrest in far-flung corners of the Empire, with a minimum of personnel and expense. At home, defence planning was based on the assumption that no major war could be expected within ten years. As a result, armaments and aircraft development languished. The RAF's needs were met by a handful of family firms working to traditional methods. Official research and development virtually ceased, so that successive aircraft designs only marginally advanced performance. Friction with France in the early 1920s resulted in a force of short-range aircraft orientated to face the perceived threat from across the Channel. When tensions eased, war seemed even less likely, and consequently the development and expansion of the force slowed even further. As for the population at large, a climate of near hysteria over the destructive effects of aerial bombing, fuelled by wildly exaggerated official reports and casualty predictions, characterised the period. In 1932 the Prime Minister, Stanley Baldwin, famously informed the 'man in the street' that 'there is no power on earth that can protect him from being bombed. Whatever people may tell him, the bomber will always get through.' Such sentiments prompted various attempts to restrict aerial bombing by international agreement, but the failure of the League of Nations' long-winded World Disarmament Conference became academic when Adolf Hitler came to power in 1933 and set Germany on the path to rearmament.

Belatedly, Britain was compelled to follow suit when it was found that Hitler was devoting huge resources to his armed forces, especially the re-emergent Luftwaffe. There was a great deal of ground to make up. The lean and wasted years of the 1920s had left the RAF equipped with unsuitable aircraft types and a vague theory of the supremacy of the bomber as a weapon. Successes against rebel tribes in Iraq and the North-West Frontier of India provided no clue as to the efficacy of the RAF's machines or tactics against a European foe. Although its pilot training was considered the best in the world, areas such as

navigation, night flying, defensive and offensive armament were still in a primitive state, having been neglected for so long. During the last five years of peace the Royal Air Force underwent a transformation, as the Government embraced the need to match Germany both in numbers and quality. A series of eight overlapping expansion schemes provided for many new squadrons, with the emphasis on bombers, although the desire to achieve numerical parity with the Germans (whose air strength was constantly exaggerated) meant a strong first-line force was only maintained at the expense of adequate reserves and an effective training organisation.

The aircraft with which Bomber Command would be obliged to go to war were conceived in the period 1932-34, and were among the first of a new breed of all-metal monoplane bombers. The Fairey Battle and Bristol Blenheim light bombers, and the Handley Page Hampden, Vickers Wellington and Armstrong Whitworth Whitley 'heavies' would all enter squadron service in 1937 or 1938, by which time most were already obsolescent, such was the pace of aircraft and aero-engine development in this period. Nevertheless, they represented a huge advance on the primitive biplane types with which the RAF had previously been equipped, and which differed little from those used during the Great War. Although far from ideal, these new aircraft — with the exception of the Battle which was obsolete even before hostilities began — would form the backbone of Bomber Command in the first two years of the war and afterwards go on to serve usefully in secondary roles.

In 1936 the old Air Defence of Great Britain organisation of the RAF, with its geographical area structure and combined functions, was swept away, and separate Bomber, Fighter and other Commands were established. Work began on a host of new airfields in eastern England, as Bomber Command was reorientated to face the new threat from Germany over the North Sea. The 'shadow factory' scheme was established to expand aircraft production, easing the strain on the circle of existing firms which could not cope with the volume of expansion, or the new production methods and technologies required for the new types. Of crucial significance for the future, in that year the Air Ministry, now convinced of the need for still larger aircraft, issued requirements for a new generation of heavy bombers, vastly more complex and advanced than had hitherto existed. True to Trenchard's doctrine, these aircraft were intended to wage an independent and decisive strategic offensive against Germany from bases in Britain. From these specifications would emerge a celebrated trio of aircraft: the Short Stirling, Handley Page Halifax and — ultimately — that most famous and successful of all bombers, the Avro Lancaster.

The threat from Hitler also necessitated a closer examination of the offensive doctrine that had dominated RAF thinking for so many years. The theoretical principle of the supremacy of bombing as a weapon had to be converted into concrete operational plans and orders for use in time of war. In 1937 a list of target priorities was drawn up by Air Ministry planners which took into account predictions of future RAF and enemy strengths and dispositions. Known as the Western Air (WA) Plans, they covered a wide range of possible objectives, the three most important being attacks on the German Air Force in its western bases, and on the industry which supported it (WA.1); attacks on the German Army's rail, road and canal communications as a means to disrupt its advance in a future invasion of France and the Low Countries (WA.4); and attacks on German industry and oil supplies, especially in the Ruhr Valley region (WA.5). However, once these and the other plans were subjected to close scrutiny by Bomber Command, it soon became apparent that the associated operational difficulties rendered the majority of them unworkable.

The attack on the Luftwaffe specified in WA.1 was essentially a defensive measure to counter the feared 'knockout blow' by enemy bombers against the urban population, which had dominated thinking for many years. The accepted wisdom had been that a strong offensive force, rather than defensive fighters, was the best deterrent against such an attack, and the first duty of the RAF, should war come, was to deliver a knockout blow of its own. Yet analysis of the problems involved, such as actually finding scores of advanced airfields and penetrating enemy airspace to attack the aircraft factories, resulted in sombre predictions of wasted effort and unsustainable losses. Plans to attack the German Army's communications, as laid out in WA.4, were even more unpopular. Besides the operational difficulties, neither Bomber Command nor the Air Staff wished to see the bomber force become embroiled in a long campaign in support of the Army, when it had been designed all along for a strategic role. WA.5, a decisive blow against industrial targets in the Ruhr, found greater favour as an effective way to damage Germany's war machine. Prime targets included power-generating plants and the highly developed synthetic oil industry, both based on Germany's bountiful supplies of high-grade coal. The Ruhr dams, and the canal and rail system connecting the region with the rest of Germany, were also identified as vital objectives. Yet, if the strategy was sound, the practical problems of penetrating the Ruhr in daylight to achieve the required degree of precision put the plan quite beyond the capabilities of Bomber Command.

Air Chief Marshal Sir Edgar Ludlow-Hewitt, appointed Air Officer Commanding-in-Chief of Bomber Command in September 1937, was only too aware of the limitations of his force and became its most outspoken critic. Among his concerns was the desperate need for navigational aids, which would enable his bombers to operate safely at night and in poor weather, and major improvements in all areas of crew training. The Munich Crisis in the summer of 1938 dramatically revealed the lamentable state of his Command. Few of the mobilised bomber squadrons were deemed ready for operations, and many deficiencies in training were brought to light. In the new climate of urgency following the crisis there was a marked improvement in aircraft production as new funds became available, but it was far too late to remedy the lack of operational efficiency. The C-in-C bemoaned in particular the standard of air gunnery, which he saw as the main weakness of his force. It was widely hoped that a formation of aircraft would be able to defend itself in daylight, but in May 1939, with the war only months away, he noted grimly that the 'weakest point of our bomber force at this moment lies in its gun defence...I fear that the standard of efficiency of air gunners and their ability to resist hostile attack remains extremely low.'

Although not all the senior airmen shared Ludlow-Hewitt's bleak assessment of the situation, enough doubt had crept in to force a reappraisal of just what Bomber Command could realistically achieve in the event of war. The answer, it seemed, was very little. Fortunately, the Government had already decided to issue bombing restrictions, whereby only military targets where there was no risk to civilians could be attacked, which in effect meant that only attacks on German naval vessels at sea or action in direct support of the British Army would be attempted. In view of Bomber Command's increasingly apparent shortcomings, the Air Staff were quite happy to accede to this policy. Conservation of the force would be the guiding principle now, at least until new aircraft and equipment were available. By now, attention had focused on Fighter Command and the defensive radar system which had been developed to control the aerial defence of Britain. The RAF retained its ultimate faith in the strategic offensive, but as the countdown to war continued, the expansion of the fighter force had become the most pressing need. It would be ironic that after two decades of espousing Trenchard's doctrine of the primacy of the bomber, the RAF's finest hour would be delivered in the summer of 1940 by the Spitfires and Hurricanes of Fighter Command.

Right:
Although the RAF had to make do with ageing biplane bombers for much of the 1930s, the Air Ministry was well aware of the need for more advanced monoplanes, and specifications issued in 1932 and 1934 finally galvanised the manufacturers into tendering designs more in keeping with those of rival nations. The more successful of these would provide sterling service in the early years of the war. The first to appear was the Armstrong Whitworth Whitley, designed from the outset solely for night operations, and which entered squadron service in March 1937. The aircraft's simple, slab-sided appearance was a result of it being designed for rapid production; the high angle of incidence of its wing endowed it with a low landing speed — important at night — and also imparted a characteristic 'nose-down' attitude in flight. K4586, seen here, was the first of two prototypes produced in the spring of 1936.
ATP 8772B

Above:
The first production Handley Page Hampden, L4032, photographed at the manufacturer's airfield at Radlett, Hertfordshire, probably around the time of its maiden flight in May 1938. The second of the trio of early-war bombers to enter service, the distinctive Hampden was smaller and lighter than the Wellington and Whitley, possessing a good turn of speed and agile handling characteristics. The first squadron to equip with the type was No 49 at Scampton in Lincolnshire, which received its first aircraft in September 1938. A year later, No 5 Group had six operational Hampden squadrons, plus a further two in reserve. L4032 did not fly in anger, and was retained instead for experimental work. **MH4857**

The anticlimax that followed the outbreak of war between Great Britain and Germany on 3 September 1939 suited Bomber Command well, considering the parlous state in which it found itself. An appeal for bombing restraint by the President of the United States, Franklin D. Roosevelt, was eagerly accepted by the British and the French, the latter particularly keen not to provoke large-scale aerial attacks on its cities. Germany, too, somewhat cynically agreed to this request, but only after she had subjugated Poland. In Britain it had been feared that the start of the war would bring mass bombing attacks with, perhaps, the use of poison gas. In the event, no such attack occurred as Germany focused her attention eastwards. This provided a much needed breathing space, a period of delay, and — for some — inactivity, which would be immortalised as the 'Phoney War'. For Bomber Command, there was relief that the 'Ruhr Plan', a full-scale attack in daylight on power-generating plants in Germany's most vital industrial region, would not have to take place immediately. The Ruhr was believed to contain about 60% of Germany's key industries, and it had been planned that such an attack would be executed if Britain was subjected to mass bombing on the outbreak of hostilities, although it was feared that the losses incurred might inflict irreparable damage to the bomber force.

Bomber Command's immediate priority was to conserve itself and concentrate on training and re-equipment. Despite the prewar rearmament and expansion programmes, its front-line strength was not impressive. After discounting 13 training squadrons in No 6 Group, and seven reserve units, the Command consisted of 33 operational squadrons, of which only 17 were equipped with medium and heavy bombers — Hampdens, Wellingtons and Whitleys — suitable for attacks on Germany. The 10 Battle squadrons of No 1 Group had been despatched to their prearranged landing grounds in the Champagne region of France, from where, as the Advanced Air Striking Force (AASF), they were ready to support the British Expeditionary Force (BEF) when the expected German ground offensive began. They were joined by two Blenheim squadrons from No 2 Group which formed part of what was termed the Air Component of the BEF, to be used for tactical reconnaissance. Although expected to follow as the second echelon of the AASF, the remaining six operational Blenheim squadrons of No 2 Group were actually retained in Britain, to operate from their home bases against possible attacks through Belgium. Because of their limited endurance and bomb loads, these aircraft were considered unsuitable as instruments of the projected strategic offensive. Like the Battles, when the time came, they would have to operate in a tactical role.

Not everyone welcomed the delay in the beginning of the 'shooting war'. The Air Ministry's Director of Plans, Air Commodore J. C. Slessor, who had been pivotal in formulating Bomber Command's strategic plans before the war, bemoaned missing a chance to damage Germany while she was preoccupied over Poland. On 7 September he wrote: 'At present we have the initiative. If we seize it now we may gain important results; if we lose it by waiting we shall probably lose far more than any gain.' He suggested that much of Germany's apparent strength was a façade, and that the time was right to attack the Ruhr power-generating plants. His view was evidence of a belief that Bomber Command in 1939 was capable of inflicting a heavy and telling blow on Germany's ability to prosecute the war. Such optimism was hardly surprising, based as it was on 20 years of self-delusion over the RAF's capabilities. However, the restrictions not to bomb any targets on German soil stayed in place. Faced with these limitations, which were also inspired by a political desire not to be the first country to begin indiscriminate air warfare, Bomber Command began its long war with operations to shower Germany with propaganda leaflets and hunt down her warships at sea. With the commencement of a strategic offensive some way off, this initial period of limited operations would at least provide opportunities to test certain tactical theories. It was not known, for instance, whether aircraft would be able to penetrate enemy-controlled airspace in daylight or whether they would need to operate under the cover of darkness. The answer was not long in coming.

The first shock occurred on 4 September when formations of Blenheims and Wellingtons attacked warships off Germany's North Sea coast. The Blenheims lost five of their number to fierce anti-aircraft fire in low-level attacks on the heavy cruisers *Admiral Scheer* and *Emden* anchored in Wilhelmshaven; at least three of their inadequate bombs bounced harmlessly from the decks of the ships without exploding. The only damage inflicted was to the *Emden* when one of the Blenheims — flown, with tragic irony, by a Flying Officer H. L. Emden — crashed into it. Meanwhile, the Wellingtons failed to locate their targets off Brunsbüttel and suffered two losses of their own when they tangled with Messerschmitts. After this setback, operations against German naval units were halted and not resumed until 29 September when, in a second *débâcle*, a formation of five Hampdens from No 144 Squadron was wiped out by fighters over Heligoland. Eighteen of the 24 aircrew involved were killed.

The Blenheims of No 2 Group and the Air Component were also suffering at the hands of German fighters when they attempted daylight reconnaissance flights over Germany. Sorties

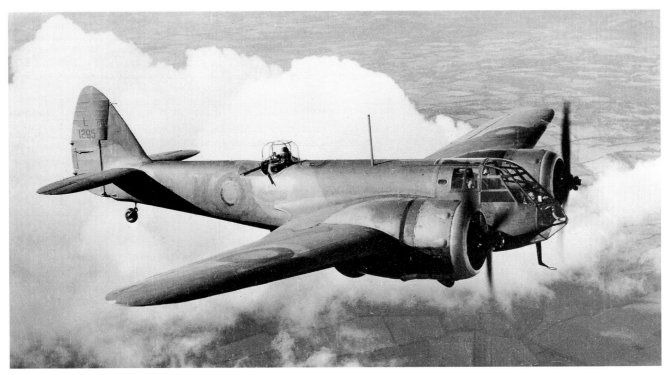

Above:
Bristol Blenheim I L1295, photographed in late 1938 or early 1939, while on strength with No 107 Squadron. The censor has obliterated the fuselage codes. The Blenheim was a development of the Bristol Type 142 high-speed passenger aircraft, sponsored by the newspaper proprietor Lord Rothermere in 1934. After humiliating the performance of contemporary RAF fighters, the aircraft was presented to the nation and ordered into quantity production as a light bomber by the Air Ministry. First entering service with No 114 Squadron in March 1937, it was, by then, rapidly becoming obsolescent and would be totally outclassed by the new generation of German fighters in 1939. Although mostly superseded by the 'long-nose' Mk IV by this date, Blenheim Is saw service with No 18 and No 57 Squadrons in France in the autumn and winter of 1939/40, as part of the Air Component of the British Expeditionary Force (BEF). During this time, ten aircraft were shot down while flying strategic reconnaissance sorties over German territory. **CH 655**

beyond the Siegfried Line in search of signs of an impending ground assault, as well as along the north German coast and over parts of the Ruhr, were proving particularly hazardous. The Battles of the AASF, probing enemy airspace across the Maginot Line on their own 'recce' flights, were found to be even more vulnerable to marauding Messerschmitts. A Battle gunner of No 88 Squadron became the first RAF airman to shoot down a German aircraft, on 20 September, but it was little consolation. Ten days later, a formation of No 150 Squadron aircraft was 'bounced' by enemy fighters and destroyed; as a result, the Battles were quickly removed from daylight reconnaissance duties. As for the other groups, operations by Wellingtons and Hampdens in search of the German Navy continued to be flown throughout October and November, with no successes, but with no further losses either as the aircraft were careful to stay well clear of the German coast to avoid interception. On 3 December, there was even a glimmer of hope that the bombers could look after themselves after all, when another formation of Wellingtons claimed a hit on a cruiser near Heligoland and successfully fought off a gaggle of Bf109s. In the process, a bomb was accidentally dropped on Heligoland itself — the first RAF bomb to be dropped on German soil.

Any hopes that this apparent success might be repeated were dashed later in the month during two famous actions, the results of which would instigate the beginnings of a sea change in Bomber Command's tactical doctrines. On 14 December, formations of Hampdens, Wellingtons and Whitleys set off over the North Sea on the biggest armed shipping reconnaissance operation so far mounted. The Wellington force, which consisted of 12 aircraft from No 99 Squadron, located and attacked a convoy in the Schillig Roads off Wilhelmshaven. Five aircraft were lost, downed by flak, it was optimistically assumed,

but in reality shot down by fighters. There was no doubt about the action on 18 December, which again involved the unfortunate Wellington squadrons of No 3 Group. In crystal clear visibility, 24 aircraft from three squadrons set off for Wilhelmshaven, following a dog-leg route along the German coast at an almost leisurely pace, tracked all the time by a recently installed, and still experimental, long-range 'Freya' radar located on nearby Wangerooge island. When the intercepting German fighters arrived on the scene, they shot down 12 out of 22 Wellingtons that had reached the target area, continuing the slaughter in a running fight out over the North Sea. These two dramatic operations, in which over half the aircraft committed were shot down or ditched on their way back, confirmed the worst fears of the C-in-C, and sent the clearest warning to those who still clung to a belief in the concept of the self-defending bomber. There were many, however, who preferred to blame inconsequential factors such as poor formation discipline and a lack of self-sealing fuel tanks, rather than face the unpalatable truth that their cherished tactical doctrines were fatally flawed.

Of all Bomber Command operations during the autumn and winter of 1939, by far the most successful — and least costly — were the leaflet-dropping flights carried out by the Whitley squadrons of No 4 Group. The only aircraft in the force designed from the outset for night operations, the slow, but capacious, Whitleys were the obvious choice for this work. The first 'Nickelling' sorties, as they were officially codenamed, were despatched on the very first night of the war and continued for the rest of the year. On the night of 1/2 October, Whitleys of No 10 Squadron unloaded their harmless cargoes over Berlin, gaining the distinction of being the first Bomber Command aircraft to fly over the German capital. The main problem during these long flights was hazardous weather, especially severe icing, which not only made conditions miserable for the crews, but also caused the very few losses that were incurred. Only four aircraft failed to return during this period, an indication of the lack of any airborne defences over Reich territory at this early part of the war. Uncomfortable though they may have been, the long 'Nickelling' sorties provided vital operational experience of navigating over blacked-out Europe, often in marginal weather conditions. Further useful experience of night operations was gained in December when No 4 Group began carrying out so-called 'security patrols' over the German Frisian Islands of Sylt, Norderney and Borkum, the object being to harass the mine-laying seaplanes that were based there. Bombs were dropped on the flare-paths and suspected mooring areas in an effort to prevent the aircraft from taking off. Occasionally, the Heinkels themselves were strafed with machine gun fire, but the strict bombing restrictions prohibited any attacks on shore installations.

By the end of the year Bomber Command had flown almost 600 sorties, but had dropped a mere 30 tons of bombs, all on naval targets. A total of 69 aircraft had been lost on operations, and a further 80 written off in accidents. Yet, apart from a limited amount of visual and photo-reconnaissance work over potential targets, the campaign against German industry had not even begun. The losses suffered in the small-scale incursions so far attempted, particularly those of December, had seriously shaken the Air Staff and Bomber Command, but the doctrine of daylight formation attacks had not yet been totally discounted. Some hoped that the larger, better-protected aircraft soon to arrive might yet succeed. Nevertheless, the dour, but realistic, Ludlow-Hewitt was now convinced of the need to consider other options, one of which was a switch to night attacks. The experiences of No 4 Group provided ample proof that night afforded the bombers vital protection. Whereas the Hampdens, Wellingtons, Blenheims and Battles had all been shot out of the sky when intercepted by the Luftwaffe, the plodding Whitleys had ranged at will over Germany, virtually invulnerable on their lonely leaflet raids. It now seemed that the rest of the Command should follow their example.

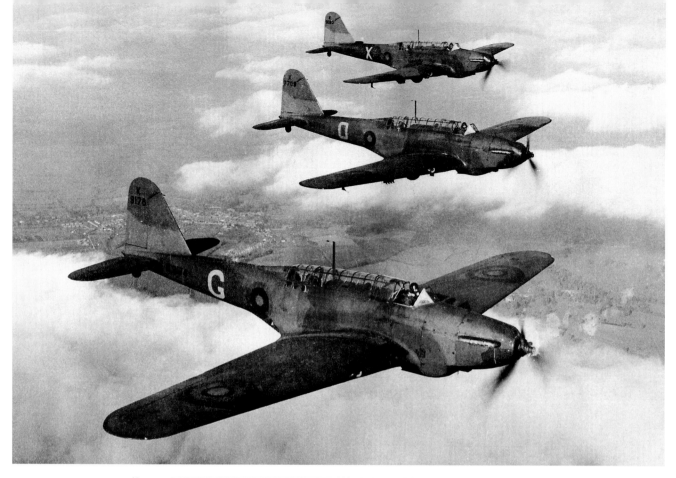

Above:
Fairey Battles of No 226 Squadron, based at Harwell in Berkshire, on a practice flight in 1939. In September of that year, the ten Battle squadrons of No 1 Group were despatched to France to become the Advanced Air Striking Force (AASF). Two of the aircraft in this photograph shared the fate of many of these hopelessly out-classed light bombers during the ensuing Battle of France: K9180/X was abandoned and set on fire during the evacuation from the squadron's airfield near Rheims on 16 May, and K9176/G failed to return from a night sortie on 20/21 May 1940. **HU 59352**

Above:
Wellington IAs and crews of No 149 (East India) Squadron at Mildenhall on 21 December 1939. One of six operational Wellington squadrons in No 3 Group, No 149 was in action from the first day of the war, taking part in searches for enemy warships off Germany's North Sea coast. These ineffectual sweeps continued without loss until the fateful 18 December, when two of its aircraft were among 12 Wellingtons shot down by enemy fighters off Wilhelmshaven. **C 423**

Left:
A close-up of another of No 149 Squadron's Wellingtons, photographed on the same occasion. The crew of a Wellington at this time normally consisted of two pilots, observer (who was also responsible for aiming the bombs), wireless operator/air gunner (WOP/AG) and rear gunner. Another gunner might also be carried to man the front turret. Despite the heavy losses among No 3 Group squadrons that December, the Wellingtons continued their daylight shipping searches over the North Sea, but were now ordered not to fly too close to the German mainland unless sufficient cloud cover was available for protection. **C 422**

Right:
An F24 camera is passed to the observer of Blenheim IV N6223/XD-Q of No 139 Squadron at Bétheniville, France, on 16 December 1939, before a reconnaissance flight over German territory. It was dangerous work; a total of 16 Blenheims were lost on 'recce' sorties between the outbreak of war and the end of the year. This particular aircraft lasted until 14 May 1940, when it was one of 13 Blenheims — including four from No 139 Squadron — shot down in attacks on German pontoon bridges over the River Meuse at Sedan. **C 116**

1940

> *These early raids were haphazard. We could choose our own route; we could bomb from any old height; sometimes we could carry whatever load we wished; we could go off at any time. We were individuals, but to tell the honest truth we were not very efficient...'*
>
> (Wing Commander Guy Gibson VC, *Enemy Coast Ahead*, 1946)

1940 was the year when Britain and her scattered Dominions stood alone. It was the year of the disastrous Norwegian and French campaigns and the so-called 'Miracle of Dunkirk'. In the late summer Fighter Command won, by the slenderest of margins, perhaps the most vital and decisive aerial campaign of World War 2. The 'Blitz' on London and other British cities began, as the Luftwaffe, hitherto more usually concerned with the tactical support of the German Army, attempted a bombing campaign of its own. Much of this has become the stuff of legend, and deservedly so, if only for the heroism and sacrifice of those caught up in misfortunes not of their own making. For Bomber Command, it was a period when the advent of its long-planned strategic offensive against Germany was repeatedly delayed by political expediency, and the demands of the tactical situation on the battlefronts. Most important of all, it was the year which saw the abandonment of daylight attacks by the heavy bomber force in favour of night operations, a general policy which would continue for the rest of the war.

The year began in the grip of the coldest winter in living memory, a factor which helped persuade Hitler to delay his attack in the West until the spring. Despite the freezing weather, Bomber Command struggled to continue its limited operations. In the middle of January, Wellingtons and Hampdens joined the leaflet offensive, flying sorties to Hamburg and Kiel. Meanwhile, the Whitleys of No 4 Group ranged ever further, reaching the distant cities of Prague and Vienna on the night of 12/13 January and Warsaw on 15/16 March. 'Nickelling' sorties would continue until April, but their prime motive now was to reconnoitre potential targets in enemy territory, and bring back information on the state of the German defences. Seaplane base security patrols also continued, carried out in the main by the Hampdens of No 5 Group, while daylight shipping searches over the North Sea were now in the hands of the Blenheims of No 2 Group. These operations met with little success, although one unexpected bonus was the sinking of a U-boat off Borkum on 11 March by a Blenheim of No 82 Squadron.

As far as future strategy was concerned, an Air Staff conference on 22 February finally agreed that the daylight Ruhr Plan should be mothballed. In the light of operational experience, it was now considered far too risky an enterprise, with forecast losses of up to 50%. Instead, priority for the strategic offensive was switched to attacks on the German oil industry, considered to be a more vital — and more vulnerable — target than the power-generating plants. Intelligence sources believed German oil stocks to be already severely depleted, and that reducing them further by bombing might have a decisive effect. Significantly, the new objectives would require attacks to be carried out at night, although at this early stage no-one yet knew whether Bomber Command could achieve the necessary level of accuracy to hit individual oil plants; the C-in-C could only stress the importance of 'night precision' training for the crews.

Some indication of the problems inherent in night bombing came from the results of Bomber Command's raid on the seaplane base at Hörnum, on the island of Sylt, on 19/20 March. This was the first time that a German land target had been deliberately attacked, in this case in retaliation for a Luftwaffe raid on the British Home Fleet at Scapa Flow. The returning Whitley and Hampden crews enthusiastically claimed to have scored numerous hits on slipways and harbour installations, and the attack was hailed as a great success. However, later reconnaissance photos showed little evidence of any damage. It was the first of many occasions when squadron operational reports, based on information supplied by the crews, found themselves at odds with the evidence supplied by photographic reconnaissance.

At the beginning of April, Air Marshal Sir Charles Portal succeeded Ludlow-Hewitt as AOC-in-C Bomber Command. He came at a time when the Air Ministry was continuing to stress the importance of the German oil industry as the primary objective for the bomber offensive. But the French, ever fearful of the power of the Luftwaffe, baulked at the prospect of initiating strategic attacks on Germany before an assault opened in the West. The British War Cabinet acquiesced to the demands of its ally, and even the Air Staff appreciated that the oil offensive might have to be a long-term strategy, especially as involvement in the defence of France and the Low Countries was looking increasingly inevitable. In the event, the first victims of German aggression in northwest Europe were Denmark and Norway. Nothing could be done for the former country, which was overrun in a single day, but attempts were made to hinder German operations in Norway by attacking airfields and naval units escorting troop convoys. The results were predictably poor — and costly. 12 April saw the largest Bomber Command raid of the war so far, when 83 aircraft struck in daylight at shipping off Stavanger. Six Hampdens from No 144 Squadron, shot down by enemy fighters, were among the nine aircraft lost. It was further proof, if any were still needed, of the perils of penetrating enemy-controlled airspace in daylight. The only course of action available to the Command had already been written into the Air Ministry directive that Portal received on 13 April: 'The operations of our heavy bombers are to be confined mainly to night action in order to conserve our force...'

The Hampden squadrons of No 5 Group flew the first Bomber Command mine-laying sorties on 13/14 April, depositing mines (which only the Hampden then had the capacity to accommodate) in the sea lanes off Denmark. 'Gardening', as this work was codenamed, would continue for the rest of the war as one of Bomber Command's most effective — and least contentious — contributions to the war effort. In time most of the 'heavies' would be involved in this regular activity, which would often be employed to introduce freshman crews to operations. As the Norwegian campaign wore on, night raids continued against shipping and airfields. Only two squadrons of Blenheims, based at Lossiemouth in Scotland, continued to fly bombing operations to Norway in daylight, attacking when sufficient cloud cover was available to evade fighter opposition. In early May, they too were withdrawn as a new crisis loomed; the invasion of France and the Low Countries was about to begin.

If Bomber Command's losses so far had been unsettling, they were as nothing compared to the tidal wave of destruction that broke at dawn on 10 May 1940. The consequences of years of neglect, disarmament and spurious tactical doctrines were finally revealed in a catastrophe of unprecedented proportions and swiftness. The Luftwaffe was at last appreciated for what it was — not a strategic force poised to flatten Paris and London, but a clinically precise instrument of support for the German Army. The German *Blitzkrieg* into France and the Low Countries was made under an umbrella of fighter protection, and the armoured spearheads were accompanied by large numbers of light anti-aircraft weapons, the effectiveness of which was soon demonstrated to the Battles and Blenheims thrown into action against the German columns. The RAF's obsolete light day bomber concept effectively died with the squadrons of hopelessly slow and poorly armed Battles of the AASF, cut down by ground fire or fighters. On 14 May the RAF suffered its heaviest day of losses so far when it carried out bombing raids against the German bridgehead over the River Meuse at Sedan; 33 Battles and 13 Blenheims were shot down or written off in crashes. Another dramatic incident occurred on 17 May when 12 Blenheims of No 82 Squadron were despatched on a raid against German armour concentrations at Gembloux in Belgium. Engaged by flak and then intercepted by Messerschmitt Bf109s, only one aircraft — badly damaged — managed to escape the ensuing slaughter. When available, RAF Hurricanes had a dramatic effect in reducing such terrible losses, but there were never enough of them and many bombing attacks had to go in unescorted.

Below:
Ground staff remove a fresh covering of snow from a Battle of No 218 (Gold Coast) Squadron, K9324/HA-B, at Aubérive-sur-Suippe, one of the AASF landing grounds near Rheims, January 1940. Despite the bitter winter weather, the squadron continued with a programme of training flights, including ground-attack and bombing exercises, during which several aircraft were lost in accidents. At the end of March they began reconnaissance and leaflet-dropping sorties over German territory, and suffered the first of many combat losses on 20 April when a Battle was shot down on a flight over the Rhine. **C 284**

Left:
The Whitley was perhaps best known for its night leaflet-dropping flights over Germany, which began on the very first night of the war. A total of 123 'Nickelling' sorties were flown before Christmas, showering Germany and the occupied territories with propaganda leaflets, at a cost of only four aircraft. In the new year, operations were extended to include such distant targets as Prague and Vienna, which were reached from forward airfields in France. Here, a member of the ground crew bids good luck to the rear gunner of a No 77 Squadron aircraft as it prepares to take off for Prague, February 1940. **C 831**

Right:
The long leaflet flights over Germany and further afield exposed crews to bitter cold, with frostbite a constant hazard. After a nine-hour sortie to Prague, this No 77 Squadron Whitley WOP/AG thaws out with a cup of hot chocolate at Villeneuve, near Paris, February 1940. Only the Whitley had the range to reach the furthest targets deep in occupied Europe, but such long trips proved to be feats of endurance for men and machines alike. **C 832**

While attention has always focused on the gallant but futile operations of the day bombers, the night force was also involved from the beginning of the French campaign, mainly in attacks on German road and rail communications behind the battlefront. As the Government, now led by Winston Churchill, prevaricated over the strategic offensive, raids were restricted by political order to targets west of the Rhine. On the night of 10/11 May, 36 Wellingtons and nine Whitleys struck at bridges across the Rhine at Wesel and military transport near Goch. Similar attacks followed, always involving small numbers of aircraft flying singly, the raids being spread over several hours. Eventually, after the Germans bombed Rotterdam on 15 May, the War Cabinet sanctioned Bomber Command raids east of the Rhine, paving the way for the long-delayed assault on Germany's industrial heart to begin at last. That night 99 bombers went to a variety of industrial, oil and rail targets in the Ruhr; it was the RAF's first strategic bombing raid of the war.

Air Marshal Portal received another directive on 4 June, one of several during his short period in charge of Bomber Command, as the Air Ministry planners sought to keep up with the fluctuating strategic situation. Once again, the C-in-C was told to concentrate on oil when moonlight allowed, on darker nights turning to the 'general dislocation of German war industry'. It was, however, appreciated that 'our strategical policy is liable to be deflected by the turn of events from the course we would like it to follow'. Indeed, the Battle of France, which was now heading towards its tragic but inevitable finale, would continue to distract Bomber Command from its efforts against oil targets throughout the first half of June. Instead, the crews found themselves despatched on operations against enemy communications and troop positions. On 10 June, with a German victory apparently near, Mussolini decided to enter the war in order to scoop a share of the spoils. This not unexpected event was met two nights later with the first Bomber Command raid on Italy. A force of 36 Whitleys, refuelling in the Channel Islands, set off on the long 1,100-mile round trip to strike at the FIAT works in Turin. For the first time, Bomber Command crews sampled the problems involved in the climb over the Alps, notably electrical storms and severe icing, which forced 23 Whitleys to turn back. One aircraft failed to return.

On 21 June, France agreed an armistice with Germany; she had been knocked out of the war in six weeks and Britain now stood alone. The Prime Minister had already told the country to brace itself for its 'finest hour'. With France gone it seemed that Bomber Command might now have a chance to devote all its resources to a potentially decisive strategic offensive against Germany. However, the immediate crisis precluded any long-term objectives. The summer of 1940 would belong to RAF Fighter Command, and once again, the bomber force was destined for a supporting role. On 20 June, Portal received a directive which changed his target priorities. With the Luftwaffe air fleets poised in bases just over the Channel in France and the Netherlands, he was now obliged to attack 'objectives which will have the most immediate effect on reducing the scale of air attack on this country'. This meant airfields, the German aircraft

industry and storage depots; secondary targets would be communications and oil plants. A subsequent directive, sent to Bomber Command at the beginning of July and inspired by the threat of invasion, placed enemy ports and shipping, especially transport barges, at the top of the target list. This was then rescinded by yet another directive on 13 July. The shopping list was now officially aircraft, oil and communications — in that order.

Whatever the targets chosen for Bomber Command, doubts were growing over the accuracy and effectiveness of night attacks. The Group Commanders themselves ventured conflicting opinions as to the standard of navigation and target-finding. Both Air Vice-Marshal Coningham of No 4 Group and Air Vice-Marshal Harris of No 5 Group claimed that their crews were proficient, whereas Air Vice-Marshal Baldwin, commanding No 3 Group, talked of 'grave limitations on night bombing of specific targets, particularly on moonless nights, owing to the inexperience of pilots and navigators in map reading by night'. Portal himself had no illusions about the chances of his crews finding and hitting distant aircraft factories at night. Widely dispersed all over Germany, and often in isolated locations, he claimed that any bombs which missed their targets (a high percentage!) would therefore hit nothing of any strategic value. Better to attack, he suggested, a district in which were concentrated many vital industrial targets, so that every bomb dropped would be of value — if only for its psychological effect. The idea of 'area bombing' against the morale of the German people had thus already taken root, at least in the mind of the Commander-in-Chief of Bomber Command.

Despite the increasingly apparent problems of finding and hitting its objectives, the summer and autumn of 1940 saw Bomber Command continuing its night attacks in accordance with the directives; on oil and communications targets when circumstances permitted, but with a substantial effort directed against airfields, aircraft factories and barge concentrations. Raids still involved small numbers of aircraft (miniscule by later standards) dispersed over several targets in a night. Routes to the targets, take-off times and bombing altitudes were all left to the discretion of individual aircraft captains. However, with an almost total dependence on 'dead reckoning' navigation, and only limited help from radio bearings and astro-navigation when conditions allowed, many aircraft strayed off course, and the bombing was widely scattered. Bad weather or ground haze, the latter common over industrial targets, accentuated the problems. The few bombing cameras available brought back disconcerting evidence that flew in the face of the reports of returning crews, but which was not conclusive enough to dent the optimistic assessments of Bomber Command's capabilities.

Once crews had successfully located their targets, attacks were often pressed home with great courage. On 12/13 August, 11 Hampdens of Nos 49 and 83 Squadrons made a daring low-level attack against two aqueducts on the Dortmund-Ems canal near Münster. As a vital transport link between the Ruhr and northern Germany, the canal was a favoured target that had been

Right:
Perched rather precariously, engine fitters work on the port Merlin X of a Whitley V of No 102 (Ceylon) Squadron at Driffield in Yorkshire, March 1940. The Whitley's slow operational cruising speed of around 140mph was not considered a handicap since German aerial opposition at night was virtually non-existent. On the night of 19/20 March, seven aircraft of the squadron joined a force of 50 Whitleys and Hampdens despatched to bomb the seaplane base at Hörnum on the island of Sylt, off Germany's North Sea coast. This operation, the biggest of the war so far, was the first bombing attack on a German land target. One Whitley — from No 51 Squadron — was lost. **C 918**

Left:
Like the other five Whitley squadrons of No 4 Group, No 102's usual activity during the 'Phoney War' was 'Nickelling'. Here, leaflets are loaded into Whitley N1386/DY-P in preparation for another 'bump' raid over Germany. Despite the dubious value of leaflet-dropping as a propaganda weapon, these operations provided bomber crews with valuable experience of extended night flying over enemy territory. Also, useful visual reconnaissance of potential targets in Germany was obtained when weather conditions allowed. **C 922**

Opposite:
The crew of another Whitley of No 102 Squadron pose for the official photographer before taking off on a leaflet raid. A five-man Whitley crew at this time comprised two pilots, observer, and two WOP/AGs. Note the one-piece Sidcot flying suits which were a feature of this period, but declined in popularity as the war progressed. The man on the right is also wearing an Irvin Harnessuit, a jerkin which incorporated a life-jacket and harness to which a parachute pack was clipped. **C 925**

attacked on several occasions before, and was destined to be attacked many more times in the next five years. On this occasion, two aircraft had already been shot down by the strong flak defences before the Hampden of Flight Lieutenant Roderick Learoyd commenced its run in. Blinded by searchlights and riddled by shell hits, Learoyd held his course and successfully dropped his bombs, which scored a direct hit, breaching the canal. He was awarded the first of 19 Victoria Crosses to go to members of Bomber Command in World War 2. No less courage was required for the long trip to Berlin, which the Prime Minister was keen to hit in retaliation for German raids on British cities. On 25/26 August the War Cabinet authorised the first bombing raid on the German capital, which was carried out by approximately 50 Hampdens. Thick cloud prevented accurate bombing and most bombs fell outside the city, much to the amusement of the German newspapers. A month later, a more concentrated attack was mounted, with over 100 aircraft raiding the city and the results were better, though still only pin-pricks by later standards.

By the end of September, Fighter Command had won the Battle of Britain, earning its place in history. The Luftwaffe had failed to destroy the RAF, and had now turned its attention to Britain's cities. While the threat of invasion remained, Bomber Command was directed on 21 September to maintain its attacks on merchant vessels and barges in enemy ports. The German aircraft industry, submarine works and communications were

also on the target list, but the Air Ministry made it clear that oil supplies should 'remain the basis of our longer term offensive strategy directed towards the disruption and dislocation of the German war potential'. On 30 October the importance of the oil offensive was again stressed, this time to Air Marshal Sir Richard Peirse, who had taken over the reins of Bomber Command when Portal was elevated to become Chief of the Air Staff at the beginning of the month. The invasion threat had receded, and significantly, the Air Ministry now decided that the time was right to 'make a definite attempt with our offensive to affect the morale of the German people when they can no longer expect an early victory...'.

In the last three months of 1940 there was a greater emphasis on targets in Germany, including some concentrated attacks during the most moonlit periods of each month. On 15/16 November, in a particularly successful raid, 67 aircraft were despatched to Hamburg, inflicting considerable damage to the Blohm & Voss shipyard, killing 26 and 'bombing-out' a further 1,625 people. The next night 130 bombers visited the city again,

Below:
The New Zealand High Commissioner, Mr W. J. Jordan, meets a Wellington crew of the New Zealand Flight at Feltwell on 20 March 1940. The New Zealanders had originally come to Britain in 1939 to pick up a batch of Wellingtons ordered by their government. When war intervened they and their aircraft were placed at the disposal of the RAF, establishing themselves as part of No 3 Group in January 1940. On 27/28 March, they flew their first operational sorties, when three Wellingtons were despatched on leaflet raids over Germany. **C 1025**

Above:
British attempts to oppose the German invasion of Norway saw a further extension of Bomber Command's range of operations. Only southern Norway could be reached, which involved long 600-mile flights entirely over water, and often in bad weather, to attack airfields and maritime targets. On 9 April, 24 Hampdens from No 5 Group set out to bomb shipping off Bergen and claimed several hits. Here, crews and aircraft of No 50 Squadron at Waddington, Lincolnshire, line up proudly shortly after the raid, which was launched from Kinloss in Scotland. **C 1180**

causing further damage and casualties. Yet, despite the inclusion of enemy morale as an objective in the latest directive, the only consciously planned area attack to take place before the year was out was that against Mannheim in the middle of December. Although the Air Staff may have preferred the idea of precision bombing in favour of general attacks, the capabilities of Bomber Command were such that little else was possible. Portal had already claimed that the destruction of workers' housing (and presumably of the workers themselves) as a by-product of attempts to hit specific industrial targets might now be accepted as a viable end in itself.

Overwhelming evidence was now mounting to convince all that night precision attacks on oil targets were virtually ineffectual. Photograph reconnaissance sorties in December brought back incontrovertible proof that the bombing results were falling far short of expectations. Photographs of two synthetic oil plants at Gelsenkirchen in the Ruhr, which had supposedly received a drenching of 260 tons of high-explosives, showed hardly any damage at all. Even more worrying, examination of the results of the first deliberate area raid on Mannheim revealed that, even here, the bombing had been widely dispersed. Air Vice-Marshal Coningham of No 4 Group had by now changed his tune concerning the capabilities of the

Above:
This No 50 Squadron crew, pictured on the wing of their Hampden, claimed to have hit a cruiser on the Bergen raid of 9 April. Of interest is the twin Vickers gas-operated (VGO) 'K' gun mounting. No less a figure than Air Vice-Marshal Arthur Harris, at that time AOC of No 5 Group, personally commissioned a private engineering firm to produce replacements for the awkward single gun mountings in his group's Hampdens, in an effort to improve their poor defensive firepower. The aircraft remained acutely vulnerable, however, and the loss of six Hampdens (and three Wellingtons) to fighters during a raid on shipping at Kristiansand on 12 April finally convinced the Air Staff of the utter futility of sending the bombers out in daylight. **C 1177**

force under his command, admitting that 'for my part, I have little idea of what the Whitleys do, and it causes me considerable anxiety'. As this momentous year drew to a close, an appreciation of the true effectiveness of Bomber Command was now dawning, and causing many others similar anxiety. It would be a while longer, though, before the situation forced a change in operational strategy.

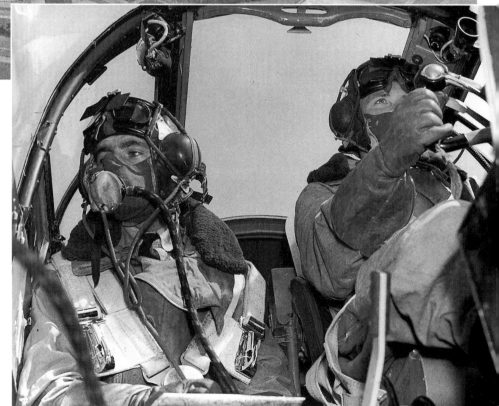

Above:
A Blenheim IV, L8756/XD-E, of No 139
Squadron over France, April 1940. No 139
was one of two Blenheim squadrons of
No 2 Group (the other was No 114) sent to
France to join the AASF at the beginning
of December 1939. Four others were
attached to the Air Component of the BEF.
All were used for strategic reconnaissance
over German territory west of the Rhine.
This aircraft survived its time with the
squadron, being pensioned off to No 9 Air
Observers School, and then No 12 (Pilots)
Advanced Flying Unit, before being struck
off charge in May 1944. **C 1309**

Above:
Observer and pilot of another No 139 Squadron Blenheim, 'on their way to
photograph enemy fortifications', April 1940. In reality the photograph was
taken on the ground. The shot shows to advantage the crew's Type B leather
flying helmets, Type D cloth oxygen masks and Mk IV goggles, all of which
were standard equipment at this time. It was a Blenheim crew of No 139
Squadron that flew the very first Bomber Command operation — a
reconnaissance flight over the North Sea and Germany — on the first day of
the war. In May 1940, the squadron would be virtually wiped out in a day
during the German *Blitzkrieg*. **C 1317**

Above:
When the German *Blitzkrieg* was unleashed against France and the Low Countries on 10 May 1940, the destruction of the AASF and Air Component began. This Battle, L5190/PH-P of No 12 Squadron, was lost on the first day of the offensive, hit by anti-aircraft fire ('flak') during attacks on advancing German troops, and crash-landing near the target. Its crew were taken prisoner. The aircraft was one of 24 Battles shot down or damaged beyond repair that day. The photograph was taken in August of that year as local German troops inspected the wreck, long after the tide of war had passed. **HU 61411**

Above:
A salvo of RAF bombs bursts in the River Meuse, near the already demolished road bridges in the centre of Maastricht, 12 May 1940. A German pontoon bridge can be seen on the extreme right. On this fateful day the Blenheim and Battle squadrons launched intensive attacks against river and canal crossings in and west of the city, in a desperate attempt to stem the German advance. Losses to flak and fighters were horrendous. In the most famous action, five Battles from No 12 Squadron, led by Flying Officer D. E. Garland (who would be posthumously awarded the Victoria Cross) were shot down attacking bridges over the Albert Canal at Veldwezelt and Vroenhoven, and the Blenheims of Nos 15, 107 and 139 Squadrons lost no fewer than 18 of their number. A further 10 aircraft were shot down in other operations before the day was out. **C 1583**

Left:
In typical early-war style, Whitley pilots and observers of No 58 Squadron gather informally round a map table to be briefed by the Station Commander on the coming night's operation, Linton-on-Ouse, Yorkshire, late May 1940. While the Battle of France was being fought and lost in daylight, the RAF night bombers did what they could with sorties against enemy road and rail communications behind the front. On 15 May, following the German raid on Rotterdam, bombing restrictions were finally lifted, and Bomber Command was given the go-ahead to attack industrial targets east of the Rhine, thus beginning the RAF's strategic offensive against Germany. **CH 218**

Right:
Aircrew of No 58 Squadron display the defensive armament of one of their aircraft. Weapons were routinely removed from aircraft between sorties for cleaning and storage. Four are holding the .303in Browning machine guns which equipped the Nash & Thompson power-operated rear turret, giving the Whitley the most powerful rear armament of any aircraft of its day. The LeadingAircraftman WOP/AG, second from right, has the single .303in VGO 'K' gun from the front turret. The practice of recruiting wireless operators and gunners on a part-time basis from volunteer ground tradesmen persisted into the early months of the war, but in June 1940 it was decreed that all aircrew should be permanent with the minimum rank of Sergeant. **CH 238**

Above:
The crew of another Whitley struggle into flying kit in front of their aircraft. On 11/12 May, No 58 Squadron participated in the first RAF raid of the war on a German town, when Bomber Command attacked communications in and around Mönchengladbach. The Whitley, one of the RAF's 'forgotten bombers', was the true workhorse of Bomber Command in the first year and a half of the war and could carry the heaviest bomb load — up to 7,000lb — of any type in use. **CH 242**

Above:
The strain shows on the faces of these Battle crews of No 226 Squadron, photographed in France at Faux-Villecerf, in early June 1940.
Evacuation of AASF squadrons to Britain was already underway, and the last Battle operations were flown on 15 June after 36 days of almost continuous action. In all, some 125 Battles were lost in action, with many more being abandoned in France. Unlike many of its kind, the aircraft in the background, L5468, escaped the attrition and went on to be transferred to the Royal Canadian Air Force in March 1942. **C 1700**

Above:
A replacement fuel tank is heaved into position during repairs to a damaged Blenheim IV of No 110 (Hyderabad) Squadron at Wattisham, Suffolk, June 1940. Experience during the French campaign revealed that the Blenheim could withstand a surprising amount of punishment. Nevertheless, losses on the squadron — as in the rest of No 2 Group — were heavy. Between the opening of the German *Blitzkrieg* in the West and the fall of France, No 110 lost 13 aircraft to enemy action. **CH 369**

Left:
The four-man crew of a Handley Page Hampden of No 83 Squadron climb from their aircraft at Scampton, June 1940. After a short detachment to Coastal Command in February and March when it operated from Lossiemouth, No 83 Squadron attacked its first ground targets in April, but over half its operations that month were mine-laying sorties. In May and June, in common with the rest of Bomber Command's night force, the squadron was thrown into the desperate attempts to stem the German onslaught in France. **CH 256**

Above:
This Whitley, N1375/DY-N of No 102 Squadron, suffered flak damage to its hydraulic system over Ludwigshafen on 20/21 June 1940, and was forced to make an emergency belly-landing at Manston in Kent. Pilot Officer W. C. McArthur and crew escaped injury. It is seen here being dismantled in preparation for transport by road to a maintenance unit. **CH 407**

Above:
In early summer sunshine, armourers prepare to load Hampden P1333/EA-F of No 49 Squadron with 250lb and 500lb general purpose (GP) bombs, Scampton, June 1940. The Hampden, which equipped the Lincolnshire-based squadrons of No 5 Group, had an official maximum bomb load of 4,000lb, but half that amount was more usually carried. On the night of 3/4 June, Bomber Command launched its largest effort to date, with 48 Hampdens among 142 aircraft sent to industrial and communication targets throughout Germany. This particular aircraft would fail to return from operations on the night of 16/17 August. **CH 263**

Above:
The New Zealand Flight at Feltwell formed the basis of a new No 75 (New Zealand) Squadron which officially came into existence on 4 April 1940. It was the first of many Allied and Commonwealth units to be formed in Bomber Command. On 17/18 April the squadron launched its first bombing attack of the war when it despatched three Wellingtons to bomb Stavanger airfield in Norway. In this photograph, taken in June at Hucknall, Nottinghamshire, the wireless operator and observer of one of the squadron's Wellingtons pose for the official photographer, while still safely on the ground. **CH 473**

Left:
A Handley Page Hereford and, flying overhead, a Hampden of No 14 Operational Training Unit (OTU), formerly No 185 Squadron, at Cottesmore, Rutland, June 1940. The OTUs were officially created from the 'Group Pool' squadrons of No 6 (Training) Group in April 1940, and were intended to provide new pilots and crews with training on the type of aircraft they would fly when posted to operational squadrons. No 14 OTU provided crews for the Hampden squadrons of No 5 Group. The Hereford was identical to the Hampden except for its unreliable Napier Dagger engines. Consequently, only a handful entered service, to be used by No 14 OTU and the other Hampden training unit, No 16 OTU at Upper Heyford. **CH 269**

Right:
Engine fitters overhaul one of the Bristol Pegasus XVIII radial engines of a No 37 Squadron Wellington at Feltwell, July 1940. The seniority in age of the 'erk' (as all junior RAF ground staff were known) on the left is apparent. The skill of prewar-trained ground crews in this early-war period meant that 'early returns' of aircraft through mechanical failure were rare, a situation that would change for the worse over the next few years as Bomber Command underwent a massive expansion. **CH 513**

Below:
Trainee Polish air gunners receive instruction on a VGO 'K' gun at an unidentified bombing and gunnery school, July 1940. These were some of the Polish airmen who had escaped to Britain after the Battle of France, some of whom had been serving with the French Air Force. In July and August, four Polish squadrons were formed in Bomber Command, equipped initially with Battles but later converting to Wellingtons. The first operational sorties were carried out by the Battles of Nos 300 and 301 Squadrons in mid-September against German barge concentrations in the Channel ports. Note the Polish eagle cap badges and the emblem on the pilot's breast pocket. **CH 573**

Above:
A busy hangar scene at No 10 OTU at Abingdon, Berkshire, July 1940, as maintenance work is carried out on a Whitley III. No 10 OTU was formed in April 1940 by the merger of two training squadrons from No 6 Group (Nos 97 and 166). The front-line squadrons of No 4 Group were by now flying the definitive Merlin-engined Whitley V, but earlier versions were still used for training, including these Mk IIIs powered by Armstrong Siddeley Tiger radials. **CH 683**

Left:
Another view of activity at No 10 OTU. A Fordson tractor pulls a train of practice bombs and armourers out to a waiting aircraft. A Whitley can be seen in the background. At this time No 10 OTU had an establishment of 54 Whitleys and 18 Avro Ansons. At the end of July it was decided that crews at the end of their training should be despatched on short operational flights to gain further experience, before being sent to a front-line unit. These usually consisted of leaflet raids over occupied France, but later OTU sorties would include bombing and mine-laying as well. **CH 674**

Above:
A gunner's view of a formation of Hampdens of No 14 OTU, based at Cottesmore, in July 1940. The Hampden's narrow fuselage design was intended to reduce drag, but meant cramped accommodation for the crew, and also created a severe handicap in that no power-operated gun turrets could be fitted. As a result, defensive armament was limited to wholly inadequate hand-operated machine guns. Hampden L4201/GL-T in the foreground was midway through an eventful career; after service with No 185 Squadron and then No 14 OTU, it was converted to a torpedo-bomber and operated by Coastal Command. **CH 709**

Right:
Wellington IAs, formerly of No 215 Squadron and now part of No 11 OTU, at Bassingbourn, Cambridgeshire, 22 July 1940. Fitters are hard at work on the port engine of the foreground aircraft while others are being warmed up for a flight. The aircraft are still wearing their old squadron codes ('LG') and have unusually large red, white and blue vertical fin flashes; units exhibited a variety of styles before the markings were standardised later in the year. Wellington IAs were fitted with retractable 'dustbin' ventral gun turrets, a next-to-useless installation omitted from later marks in favour of manually-operated, window-mounted 'beam' guns. **CH 766**

Above:
A Blenheim IV and crew of No 40 Squadron at Wyton, Huntingdonshire, 22 July 1940. The dorsal turret is equipped with a single VGO 'K' gun, which was utterly inadequate compared to the weapons carried by enemy fighters. Subsequent modifications to the Blenheim included a new Bristol Mk IV gun turret with twin .303in Browning machine guns, in an attempt to give the gunner more hitting power. Blenheim units also experimented in the field with various armament 'lash-ups' including rearward-firing guns in the upper engine nacelles and under the rear fuselage. Despite such improvements, the aircraft remained extremely vulnerable and depended on cloud cover to provide some measure of protection, especially when on unescorted sorties. **CH 717**

Left:
More No 40 Squadron Blenheims at Wyton, this time on 26 July 1940. Despite the horrendous losses suffered by No 2 Group during the Battle of France in May and June, the Blenheim force was quickly replenished. By the end of July, 11 squadrons with 180 aircraft were available. They continued to operate, mostly in daylight, against airfields, barge concentrations and coastal batteries. From 21 June sporadic raids were also mounted on industrial targets in Germany, in a vain effort to force the enemy to dissipate his fighter defences. L9402/BL-U, in the middle distance, went on to serve with No 139 Squadron, until it was written off after colliding with another aircraft returning from an attack on Den Helder on 28 February 1941. **CH 753**

Right:
Battles from No 12 OTU at Benson, Oxfordshire, flying in 'vic' formation, July 1940. Most of the obsolete Battles had finished their brief, but bloody, period on operations, although a re-formed No 1 Group continued to operate the type for a time against the Channel ports. The last operational Battle sorties were flown by nine aircraft on 15/16 October against invasion barges at Calais and Boulogne. For the remainder of the war the aircraft would serve successfully in the training role, mainly at the Bombing and Gunnery Schools at home or overseas as part of the Commonwealth Air Training Plan. **CH 772**

Below:
At the end of July 1940, the Commander-in-Chief of Bomber Command, Air Marshal Sir Charles Portal, visited Wyton to invest 15 NCO aircrew with the Distinguished Flying Medal. Among the recipients — mostly observers and air gunners — on parade here is wheelchair-bound Sergeant G. A. Gamble, a No 40 Squadron Blenheim gunner who was wounded fighting off an attack by Messerschmitt Bf109s over the Netherlands on 27 June. His aircraft, though damaged, escaped to crash-land at the fighter aerodrome at Hawkinge in Kent. **CH 777**

Above:
A Douglas DB-7 Boston I, AE458, is readied for an inspection by the Duke of Kent during a display of new aircraft types at the Aeroplane & Armament Experimental Establishment (A&AEE), Boscombe Down, Wiltshire, on 28 August 1940. Although British orders for the American-built light bombers had been placed earlier in the year, the RAF's first Bostons were acquired from consignments originally intended for the French. The first batch to arrive in Britain were designated Boston Is and were used for pilot training. Most of the Boston IIs that followed were converted into night-fighter and intruder variants — called Havocs. The Boston III light bombers specifically ordered for the RAF would not arrive until the following year.
CH 1108

Left:
A trainee wireless operator practises his craft at No 10 OTU at Abingdon, August 1940. The radio set has been mounted in a special cubicle, known as the 'Harwell Box', to simulate its position in a bomber. Above is the direction-finding (D/F) loop which was mounted on top of the aircraft's fuselage. With the door shut, the airman was given some idea of operating in a darkened aircraft interior. At this stage of the war, wireless operators were trained as air gunners as well, and their total course lasted longer than that of any other crew member.
CH 1275

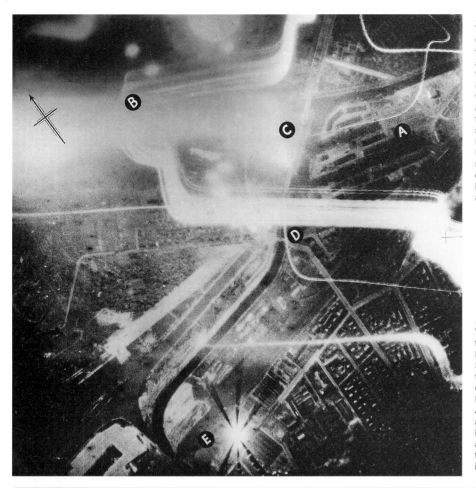

Left:
The first photograph released of a Bomber Command attack on Berlin, probably taken on the night of 23/24 September 1940 when 129 aircraft were concentrated against various targets within the city. The Verbindungs Canal is visible running from bottom left to top right, with the Westhafen inland docks marked at 'A' and the Charlottenburg gas-holders at 'E'. The first raid on Berlin, on 25/26 August, had been sanctioned by the War Cabinet following Luftwaffe raids on London the previous night. Eight further raids, with varying degrees of success, were despatched to the German capital during the autumn. The broad strokes of light in the photograph are searchlight tracks and the thin ones tracer. **C 1828**

Below:
Visitors do not come any more important than this! On the evening of 27 November 1940, HM King George VI visited Nos 38 and 115 Squadrons at Marham, Norfolk, and stayed throughout the night to observe an actual operation in progress. In this photograph, the King (third from left), Air Vice-Marshal J. Baldwin, AOC No 3 Group (second from left) and Air Marshal Sir Richard Peirse, C-in-C Bomber Command (second from right), watch as members of a Wellington crew just back from Cologne struggle to concentrate during interrogation. **CH 1767**

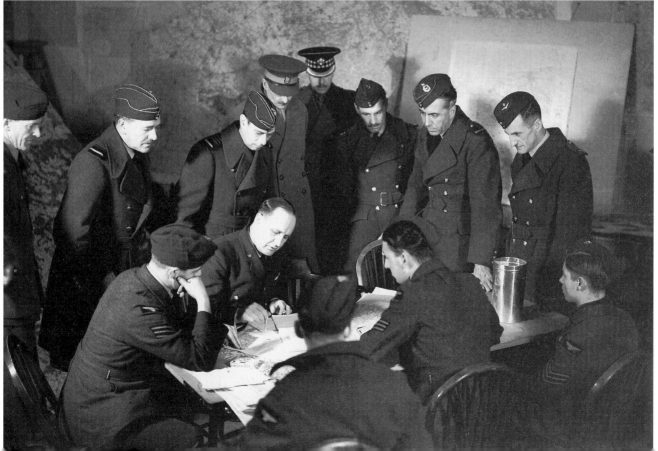

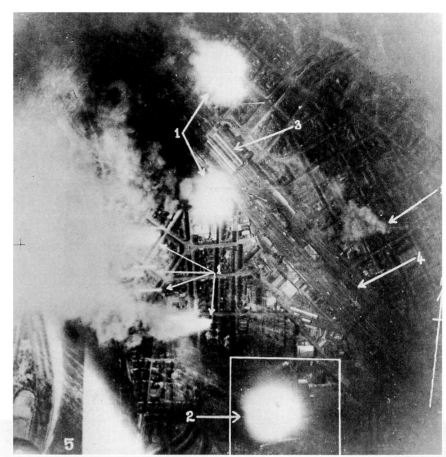

Right:
Operation 'Abigail Rachel' — Mannheim under attack, 16/17 December 1940. In retaliation for recent German raids, in particular the attack on Coventry, the War Cabinet authorised Bomber Command to target, for the first time, the centre of a city instead of specific industrial locations. The 134 aircraft sent represented the largest force yet despatched to a single target. The central railway station (3) and marshalling yards (4) are visible in this view, with the Rhine on the left (5) and large fires burning (1 & 2). Nine bombers were shot down over Germany or crashed in Britain. The bombing itself was scattered and largely ineffective, but the raid was a portent of things to come. **C 1853**

Below:
Workmen lend some muscle as a brand new Whitley V, serial number Z6462, is brought out from Armstrong Whitworth's final assembly hall at Baginton aerodrome, Coventry, on 20 December 1940. Delivered to No 58 Squadron at Linton-on-Ouse, and coded GE-D, this unfortunate Whitley was destined to last less than a month; it was shot down over the Netherlands during a raid on Wilhelmshaven on 16/17 January 1941. **E(MoS) 69**

CHAPTER 3

1941

> '...the operational experience of late 1940 and early 1941 had sufficed to convert Bomber Command from a force which had previously been mainly devoted to the aim of precision attack to one which was now predominantly concerned with area bombing.'
>
> (Official History, HMSO, 1961)

At the beginning of 1941 Bomber Command seemed, at last, to be in a position to resume its long-planned assault on Germany, free from the strategic diversions which had been such a feature during the critical year that had just passed. The threat of invasion had faded, and Britain's most immediate problem now was to continue to keep open her Atlantic sea-lanes in the face of the German U-boat and surface raider threat. With the Army — or what was left of it — safely back home and licking its wounds, there seemed little prospect of offensive action on land in the foreseeable future. Yet, in this first full year of the bomber offensive, Bomber Command's ambitions to take the war to the heart of the Reich were to be frustrated again, as more pressing priorities established themselves, and its own limitations were fully revealed. The deteriorating situation at sea was to dominate the first half of the year, while attempts to pursue a precision night campaign against industrial targets would achieve little other than to crater the fields and forests of western Germany. On the plus side, the process of re-equipment would begin, with the first of the new generation of bombers — the Stirling, Halifax and Manchester — beginning operations, albeit in very limited numbers due to technical problems. A growing and dispiriting awareness of the problems associated with night bombing would be, perhaps, the most significant factor as the year progressed. Just as 1940 had seen a major shift to night operations, 1941 would see confirmation of a further sea change in operational strategy, this time from precision to area attacks, as Bomber Command shed the last of its prewar misconceptions and faced the cold reality of the night offensive against Germany.

The Air Ministry directive sent down to Bomber Command on 15 January 1941 once again restated the German oil plants as the primary objective, despite Air Chief Marshal Portal's private belief that the future lay in the area bombing of industrial towns, and the Prime Minister's own desire for a more ruthless bombing policy. Churchill followed the progress of the bomber offensive closely, but had always been very sceptical about the Air Staff's claims as to the effectiveness of precision oil attacks. He distrusted the carefully calculated statistics and optimistic forecasts upon which so much Air Ministry attention

was focused; for him it was vital that Britain hit back hard at German cities, not only in retaliation for apparently indiscriminate bombing during the Blitz, but also because it offered the only way at that time to take offensive action against the enemy. It is doubtful whether the Prime Minister ever really saw the bomber force as a war-winning weapon on its own, but his support in a period when results were poor was crucial for Bomber Command's very survival in the face of formidable opposition from its critics.

Intelligence assessments by the Ministry of Economic Warfare had concluded that the oil position of the Axis powers had reached a critical point, a view somewhat naively accepted by Portal, who argued that the destruction of 17 major refineries and synthetic oil plants over the next six months would cause 'a heavy and possibly fatal blow to Germany'. The January directive reasoned that as long as the present scale of air attack was maintained, the enemy's oil position would cause them 'grave anxiety' by the spring, and if increased, might 'place the enemy in a most critical position'. It was stated that destruction of the first nine of the 17 listed oil plants would reduce production by 80%. These calculations were based on grossly inaccurate assessments concerning the state of the German economy, and the effectiveness of the RAF bombing which had already taken place. In reality, fuel production had been scarcely affected by British attacks. However, now that the planners were beginning to appreciate the difficulties associated with attacks at night, especially in adverse weather conditions, the January directive advised Bomber Command that, when it was unprofitable to plan attacks against the oil objectives, it should continue 'harassing the enemy's main industrial towns and communications' and periodically mount 'heavy concentrations against the former to maintain the fear of attack'.

The winter weather was indeed proving to be the most persistent obstacle; clear visibility was the exception and only 221 sorties were flown against oil targets in the first three months of the year. The poor flying conditions were also responsible for a host of crashes. On the night of 11/12 February dense fog over airfields in England caused the loss of 22 bombers returning from Bremen, when crews had to abandon them by parachute. Despite the weather, Air Marshal Peirse managed a number of fairly concentrated attacks against key targets: on 9/10 January 135 aircraft raided Gelsenkirchen, 222 bombers went to Hannover on 10/11 February and 131 made the trip to Cologne on the first night of March. Cologne would be an oft-visited target when bad weather conditions prevented the planned attempts to pick out specific oil plants in the Ruhr. Even on the best moonlit nights, however, the bombers were often still failing to locate their objectives; on the night of 14/15 February, 44 Wellingtons were sent to the Nordstern synthetic oil plant at Gelsenkirchen, but only nine aircraft claimed to have actually dropped bombs on the target. Nowhere near enough destruction was being inflicted, even set against Portal's unrealistic estimate of 3,420 sorties required to knock out the plants. Unfortunately for its exponents, the 'Oil Plan' had hardly got off the ground before unforeseen events overtook it. In March, with a new national crisis looming, the Prime Minister intervened, and Bomber Command was diverted towards an altogether different objective.

Not for the last time, the Battle of the Atlantic now impinged on Bomber Command's plans. The successes of German U-boats, surface raiders and long-range aircraft against convoys in the North Atlantic had reached a high-point, and were threatening Britain's very survival. On 9 March, a new directive informed Bomber Command that it should devote its energies to 'defeating the attempt of the enemy to strangle our food supplies and our connection with the United States.' The Prime Minister's own words were employed: 'We must take the offensive against the U-boat and the Focke-Wulf wherever we can and whenever we can. The U-boat at sea must be hunted, the U-boat in the building yard or in dock must be bombed.

The Focke-Wulf, and other bombers employed against our shipping, must be attacked in the air and in their nests.' For the next four months, Peirse was obliged to target a selected list of French and German ports, factories associated with U-boat construction and airfields used by Focke-Wulf FW200 'Condor' maritime patrol aircraft. The battle-cruisers *Scharnhorst* and *Gneisenau* in Brest were also added to the list of objectives by verbal order. He was allowed to continue with the oil plan when weather and circumstances allowed, but, significantly, priority of selection was to be given to those targets in Germany 'which lie in congested areas where the greatest morale effect is likely to result'.

Below:
In August 1940 the first of the RAF's four-engined bombers, the Short Stirling, entered service with No 7 Squadron at Leeming. However, a host of teething problems meant that the handful of aircraft delivered were not ready for operations until the beginning of the new year, by which time the squadron had moved to Oakington in Cambridgeshire. The Stirlings finally flew their debut operation on the night of 10/11 February 1941, when three aircraft attacked oil storage tanks at Rotterdam. This aircraft, N3641/MG-D, seen preparing for a flight, was the second Stirling to be delivered to the squadron and took part in that first raid. **CH 3139**

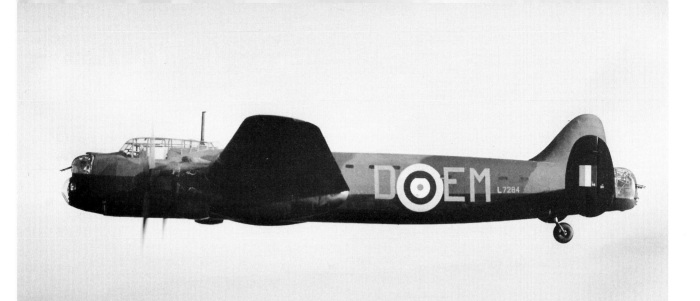

The maritime campaign which followed produced little in the way of major material damage — hardly new as far as Bomber Command was concerned — but was perhaps more valuable than the wasteful attempts to attack oil plants. The *Scharnhorst* and *Gneisenau* in dock at Brest proved extremely difficult targets to hit, but enough damage was caused to prevent either ship from venturing forth into the Atlantic again. One unfortunate effect of raids on the U-boat bases at Lorient and St Nazaire was that they prompted the Germans to begin construction of huge concrete pens, which would provide impenetrable shelters for the submarines and their vital services. The period also saw the first excursions of the new Stirling, Manchester and Halifax bombers to targets in Germany, but due to a host of teething problems and production hold-ups few of these aircraft were as yet available, and it was left to the older Whitleys, Hampdens and especially the Wellingtons to bear the brunt of the offensive. Bremen, Hamburg and Kiel received most attention, with the last attracting the largest Bomber Command raid of the war so far on 7/8 April, when 229 aircraft inflicted widespread damage in perfect moonlit conditions. Two of the three U-boat construction yards there were put out of action for several days. A follow-up raid occurred on the next night; the Air Staff directive had made it clear that, where possible, chosen targets should be subjected to successive attacks in order to compound the effects and maximise 'hardship and dislocation'. In the first half of May, Hamburg was subjected to five raids, which caused extensive damage and considerable alarm amongst the population.

While the bulk of Bomber Command was now fully committed to the night offensive, it was left to No 2 Group to maintain a daylight role. In 1940, its Blenheim crews had been sacrificed in ill-conceived daylight operations over southern Norway, France and the Low Countries; during the winter months they had been despatched on night sorties against German industrial targets and airfields in occupied Europe. With the threat of invasion gone and the strategic offensive in the hands of the heavy bombers, 1941 would see new tasks for the Blenheim force, which numbered some 150 aircraft. In January, the first 'Circus' operations were mounted, whereby small forces of aircraft penetrated enemy airspace, accompanied by a strong fighter escort. These raids were principally designed to draw the Luftwaffe into combat with the RAF fighters, but since the range of the latter limited the operations to low-value targets in northern France, there was little reason for the enemy to take the bait. In March, in response to the Prime Minister's determination to close the sea lanes around Britain to enemy vessels, No 2 Group was ordered to conduct low-level anti-shipping strikes in the Channel and North Sea. Inevitably, losses during these hazardous operations, which continued until November, were horrendous and the results paltry. They served only to highlight, once again, the uncomplaining heroism of the Blenheim crews.

By July 1941, the situation at sea was deemed sufficiently under control to release Bomber Command from its four-month maritime diversion. A new directive informed Sir Richard Peirse that he should now concentrate the efforts of his Command towards dislocating Germany's rail and canal transportation system, and attacking the morale of her civilian population, alleged to be already suffering from recent RAF raids on industrial towns. Nine rail centres in western Germany were identified as the key targets for clear, moonlit nights, the intention being to isolate the Ruhr-Rhine area from the rest of the Reich and Italy. Three of them were located in Cologne, Duisburg and Düsseldorf, congested industrial cities which were also suitable for area attack on moonless nights, when the distinctive River Rhine would aid target-finding. The Dortmund-Ems and Ems-Weser canals were also selected for attack, as were a number of more distant ports and industrial cities elsewhere in Germany. Operations against these would serve to dissipate the enemy's defences. No mention was made of the Oil Plan in this latest directive, an indication that Bomber Command's failure in this regard had been tacitly accepted by the Air Staff. It was considered that communications, especially large railway yards, were easier to hit and knock out than oil plants, and would cause as much disruption to the German economy.

Meanwhile, ignoring all the lessons of history, Hitler had invaded Russia, thus ensuring his own eventual defeat. From now until the end of the war, the vast bulk of the Wehrmacht would be bled white in the East. With much of the Luftwaffe also initially committed to this enterprise, Bomber Command was presented with new opportunities, including the possibility of increasing daylight attacks. On 26 June, Air Vice-Marshal Sir Robert Saundby, Senior Air Staff Officer (SASO) at Bomber Command, wrote that 'if we can succeed in concentrating the enemy's fighters in the Pas de Calais area, and containing them there by continuing our bombing attacks with strong fighter support, we ought to be able to create opportunities for the daylight attack of objectives in Germany and North-Western France'. It seemed that some had yet to relinquish their old faith in daylight bombing, especially since the near-impossibility of accurate night bombing was now becoming apparent. Small forces of the new four-engined bombers, which were considered to be better able to look after themselves, were now occasionaly used on 'Circus' operations, or sent on unescorted daylight cloud-cover raids. For example, on 28 June, six Stirlings attempted to hit Bremerhaven and one aircraft was lost. Two days later, one of a formation of six Halifaxes was shot down attacking targets in the same area. Such pin-prick attacks had negligible strategic value.

Major daylight raids during the summer by heavy bombers on German warships in French ports finally scotched any ideas that the Luftwaffe had left an insufficient number of fighters in the West. Despite diversionary operations in northern France and long-range Spitfire escorts, 12 bombers — mostly Wellingtons — were shot down by flak and fighters while attacking the *Gneisenau* and *Prinz Eugen* at Brest on 24 July. Even worse, 15 Halifaxes sent unescorted against the *Scharnhorst* at La Pallice on the same day were badly shot up and lost five of their number when intercepted by Messerschmitts. The strategic importance

Below:
A loaded bomb trolley makes a convenient seat for the crew of a Wellington IC of No 311 (Czechoslovak) Squadron as they pose for the photographer at East Wretham, Norfolk, February/March 1941. The squadron was formed in July 1940 at Honington from Czech personnel who had escaped to Britain before the fall of France. A unique formation in Bomber Command, the Czechs took part in 152 bombing raids at a cost of 19 aircraft before being transferred to Coastal Command in April 1942. **CH 2187**

Above:
German investigators and Luftwaffe personnel examine the rear fuselage section of a Whitley V, Z6585 of No 77 Squadron, based at Topcliffe, Yorkshire, which was shot down on an operation to Berlin on the night of 17/18 April 1941. This Whitley was one of eight bombers lost from a total force despatched of 118 aircraft. Flying Officer L. Pearson and his crew all perished. **EA 75435**

of their targets, and the vital damage which was inflicted, no doubt justified the effort and losses, but this did not alter the fact that, in the words of one Bomber Command report, 'unsupported daylight attacks by heavies when faced by equal or slightly superior numbers of fighters are not a practical proposition'. Much the same could be said to apply to the light bombers of No 2 Group, which were no less vulnerable. In the middle of August, six Blenheim squadrons lost 10 from 54 aircraft attacking power stations near Cologne, a casualty rate of over 18%. The real solution to the problem — the development of long-range escort fighters — had already been rejected by the Chief of the Air Staff, Sir Charles Portal, who assured Churchill in May that no aircraft with the required endurance would have the performance to meet the enemy's defensive fighters on equal terms. In time he would be proved very wrong on this point, but for now daylight bombing was shown to be just as impossible as it had been at the start of the war.

The daylight experiments of 1941 had merely served to confirm the hard-won lessons of 1939 and 1940. Yet, unlike the situation at the start of the war, when it was assumed that Bomber Command would be able to hit its targets accurately by night if it was prevented from doing so by day, operational experience since then had shown this to be a forlorn hope. Any lingering doubts as to the true scale of the problem were swept away by the publication in August of a report on bombing accuracy commissioned by Churchill's scientific adviser, Lord Cherwell. The report's author, a Mr D. M. Butt of the War Cabinet Secretariat, analysed 600 bombing photographs and operational summaries obtained during June and July, and his conclusions were genuinely shocking: only a third of the aircraft which claimed to have attacked a target actually got within five miles of it. This figure rose to two-thirds over the French ports but fell to one in ten over the Ruhr. Weather conditions obviously had an effect; bright moonlit nights made the job of navigation slightly easier, but even then the margin of error could be huge. Moreover, Butt's figures were derived from the results of only those crews which actually reported reaching the target; when the total number of aircraft despatched on an operation was taken into account the figures were even more disturbing. Whatever the objections to the report's statistical methods — and there were many — the unpleasant truth could no longer be ignored. At great effort and expense, Bomber Command was scattering explosives over a wide area of Germany with very little in the way of damage to show for it.

Scientific aids, now under development and almost ready for service, held out hope for a solution to the problem of night-time navigation, which was now seen as even more vital than accurate bomb aiming. Meanwhile, there was a belief that, if Bomber Command could not be a precision tool, with enough aircraft it might become an effective blunt instrument. The Air Staff proposed the construction of 4,000 bombers, a fantastic requirement, with which they promised to flatten German morale and achieve 'decisive results by imprecise means'. But such ideas did not impress Churchill, tired of mathematical forecasts, and doubtful whether German morale was any more fragile than that of the British. By now he had made up his mind that the bombing offensive might well play a major part in the eventual Allied victory, but could not win the war on its own: 'The most we can say is that it will be a heavy and I trust a seriously increasing annoyance.' To devote virtually all of

Above:
Aircrew of No 149 Squadron at Mildenhall on 1 May 1941. On the night of 31 March/1 April, during a raid on Emden, a specially modified Wellington flown by Pilot Officer J. H. Franks (centre, with moustache) dropped one of the first two 4,000lb high-capacity (HC) blast-bombs of the war. The other was dropped by a No 9 Squadron aircraft on the same target. The 'Cookie', as the weapon was popularly known, had a thin case and powerful explosive filling, and was intended to cause maximum damage to buildings. It was to become one of the most widely used and destructive devices in Bomber Command's armoury. **CH 17196**

Britain's economic resources to a weapon that had yet to prove itself, and might never do so, was simply no longer an option as far as the Prime Minister was concerned. For now, the plan was to solve Bomber Command's immediate problems, and press on with the offensive as before.

The autumn of 1941 found Bomber Command at perhaps its lowest ebb. Its front-line strength had increased only very slowly and stood at less than 400 serviceable aircraft, scarcely different from that of a year earlier. Any numerical gains from the formation of new units were being largely cancelled out by the transfer of squadrons to Coastal Command or the Middle East. Target-finding and bombing accuracy were consistently poor. The number of Manchesters, Stirlings and Halifaxes available was still insignificant as all were plagued with various teething troubles. Moreover, squadrons converting to the new types were unavailable for operations. Most worrying of all, losses were mounting sharply as the German air defence network became established and the night-fighter force showed its teeth. At the beginning of the year, Bomber Command's average loss rate had been running below 2%; now it was creeping towards double that figure. On 7/8 November, in a disastrous maximum-strength raid in treacherous weather conditions on Berlin and other targets, 37 aircraft failed to return from a force of 392 bombers — a loss rate of 9.4%. A watershed had been reached and Sir Richard Peirse was ordered by the War Cabinet to scale down operations in order to conserve his force; there seemed scant reason to fritter away crews for little or no gain. In this darkest hour for the bomber force, the only glimmer of light was provided by the imminent arrival of a much-needed radio navigation aid — called 'Gee' — and the potential of a new aircraft — the Avro Lancaster — which was about to be delivered to the squadrons. Both the Air Staff and the Government looked to 1942 to end the crisis of confidence in the strategic offensive, and to bring about a major improvement in Bomber Command's fortunes.

Above: A bomb train arrives to load up a No 149 Squadron Wellington IC at its dispersal at Mildenhall on 10 May 1941. The Wellington could carry up to 4,500lb of bombs, which allowed it an operational radius of 560 miles. That night, under a full moon, 119 bombers were sent to Hamburg and a further 23 made the trip to Berlin. With its two U-boat construction yards, Hamburg was one of the priority maritime targets against which Bomber Command directed its main effort during this period. The seven aircraft which failed to return included one from No 149 Squadron. **CH 2676**

Above: A Boeing Fortress I, AN521/WP-K of No 90 Squadron, undergoing an engine change, June 1941. This aircraft — one of 20 former US Army Air Corps B-17Cs purchased by the RAF — was the first to arrive in Britain, on 30 April 1941. No 90 Squadron, previously part of No 17 OTU, was re-formed on 7 May as part of No 2 Group to operate the Fortresses on high-altitude precision daylight attacks from Polebrook, Northamptonshire; the first raid took place on 8 July when three aircraft raided Wilhelmshaven. This particular Fortress eventually went with a detachment to the Middle East in October 1941 and was written off in a crash there in January 1942. **E(MoS) 324**

Above: Armourers of No 75 (New Zealand) Squadron pose with a pair of 500-pounders and give the 'thumbs up' in front of the 'Wellington Devil', a suitably decorated Wellington IC, Feltwell, May 1941. The solid and reliable Wellington was emerging as the mainstay of Bomber Command's force, equipping a total of 18 squadrons in Nos 1 and 3 Groups. Wellingtons were also on strength with two new squadrons formed in April within No 4 Group — No 104 and No 405 (Vancouver), the latter being the first Canadian squadron in Bomber Command. **CH 2714**

Above: Hampden AD986 of No 106 Squadron at Coningsby, Lincolnshire, June 1941. On the night of 4/5 July this aircraft and two others from the squadron failed to return from operations over the Ruhr. One Hampden was shot down over the Netherlands, another crashed in the Thames Estuary on the way back and AD986 was lost over Germany. There were no survivors from any of the aircraft. On the same night, Bomber Command's main strength was directed against Brest and Lorient for the loss of only one Whitley. **HU 42447**

Above: An Avro Manchester I, L7291 of No 97 Squadron, about to be bombed-up at Coningsby, May/June 1941. No 97 was the second unit in Bomber Command to equip with the flawed twin-engined bomber and flew its first operation on 8/9 April when four aircraft — including this one — were despatched to Kiel. Over half of all Manchesters delivered were either shot down or crashed in accidents and L7291 was destined to be one of them. Originally delivered to No 207 Squadron, it survived service with No 97 and two other operational units, before going to No 1654 Conversion Unit at Wigsley, Nottinghamshire, where it caught fire and crashed on 4 April 1943. **HU 42459**

Left:
In March 1941 the hard-pressed Blenheim squadrons of No 2 Group began their most intensive and hazardous operations to date, in the form of daylight anti-shipping strikes off the enemy-controlled coast. The intention was to disrupt all coastal shipping, initially between Brittany and Germany's North Sea coast, as part of Churchill's general order to Bomber Command to concentrate on naval targets. The sweeps were carried out at very low level — often below 50ft — within designated areas or 'beats'. Any ships sighted had to be attacked quickly and effectively, and the aircraft make good their escape, before enemy fighters arrived on the scene. The Blenheim crews pressed home their attacks with epic bravery and determination despite rapidly mounting losses. As well as flak ships and fighters, flying at 'wave-top' height brought its own hazards. This Blenheim, V6034 of No 21 Squadron, struck the mast of the ship it was attacking off the Frisian Islands and cartwheeled into the sea, 16 June 1941. **C 1939A**

Above: Stirling N3663/MG-H of No 7 Squadron, on display at Newmarket Heath, Suffolk, during a visit by King Peter of Yugoslavia in July 1941. A typical bomb load is on view beneath the aircraft for the King's inspection. This unfortunate Stirling was destined for 'the chop' only a matter of days later, when it was shot down by a night-fighter on an operation to Berlin on the night of 2/3 August. Pilot Officer C. Rolfe and two of his crew survived to become POWs. **CH 3175**

The undercarriage retraction mechanism of a No 7 Squadron Stirling is checked for smooth operation at Oakington, July 1941. The tall, spindly undercarriage of the massive Stirling was prone to collapse if the aircraft swung on take-off or landing. Unnervingly, such failures could also occur without warning to parked aircraft. Note the maintenance trestles on the right which were essential for servicing crews to reach the wings and engines of an aircraft which towered almost 23ft above the ground. **D 4741**

Below:
For a period in July 1941 Stirlings were tried out on daylight 'Circus' operations, usually undertaken by the Blenheims of No 2 Group. These incursions involved small numbers of heavily escorted bombers raiding targets in France and the Low Countries, the intention being to lure the Luftwaffe into battle with the RAF fighters. One such operation took place on 5 July, when three Stirlings of No 15 Squadron went to a steel factory at Lille. In this view from the mid-upper turret of one of the bombers, Hawker Hurricanes provide close escort on the way to the objective. However, it was flak rather than fighters that proved the main hazard for the Stirlings; that month, three aircraft were lost in two weeks while the German fighters refused to take the bait. As a result the Stirlings were withdrawn. **C 2027**

Above:

The shipping strikes begun in the spring by No 2 Group continued throughout the summer months. On 7 July 1941, Blenheims from Nos 105 and 139 Squadrons attacked a convoy of eight merchant ships between The Hague and Ijmuiden. The four escorting flak ships and one E-boat put up a murderous barrage, and two Blenheims were shot down and others holed. On the way home another Blenheim was destroyed by Bf109s. None of their crews survived. During the attack two ships were hit, including the Danish-registered *Delaware*, as seen in this dramatic photograph taken from the gun turret of one of the Blenheims. **C 1936**

Right:

On 24 July 1941 a major daylight operation was mounted against the *Gneisenau* and *Prinz Eugen* at Brest and the *Scharnhorst* at La Pallice, further down France's Atlantic coast. A force of 79 Wellingtons and 18 Hampdens, with a trio of Boeing Fortresses of No 2 Group, went to Brest. Six hits were claimed, but the Wellingtons suffered from stronger than expected fighter opposition and lost ten of their number. The Hampdens, escorted by long-range Spitfires, fared better and all but two made it back, including this aircraft of No 106 Squadron seen immediately after its return from the raid. The crew and ground staff are examining some minor flak damage. **HU 42439**

The observer at work in a Stirling of No 15 Squadron, August 1941. 'Dead-reckoning' navigation, on which the bomber crews depended, involved computing the airspeed and course of an aircraft with that of the strength and direction of forecast winds, in order to calculate the aircraft's actual track over the ground. To prevent errors caused by fluctuating winds, it was necessary for navigators to obtain frequent visual 'fixes' of their position, which at night over blacked-out Europe, perhaps with an overcast obscuring the ground, was an extremely difficult task. Darkness meant protection for the bombers but rendered them almost blind. Huge navigation errors were commonplace, especially in marginal conditions, and it was becoming increasingly apparent that most crews were missing their objectives by miles, sometimes hundreds of miles. In this period before the advent of radar aids, finding and hitting its targets, even on moonlit nights, was proving to be Bomber Command's greatest challenge. **CH 3290**

Below:
A Wellington IC of No 301 (Pomeranian) Squadron is refuelled at Hemswell in Lincolnshire, August 1941. Note the 'A' Flight marking on the tractor-towed bowser. This Polish unit had formed in July 1940 and, after a brief spell with Fairey Battles, operated Wellingtons until the squadron was disbanded in April 1943, due to a shortage of Polish crews. During its period of service with Bomber Command, No 301 Squadron flew 1,220 Wellington sorties, losing 29 aircraft and 203 aircrew killed or taken prisoner. **HU 83515**

Left:
Although the bulk of Bomber Command was committed to night attacks for the foreseeable future, it was seen as vital to maintain the capacity to launch attacks against land targets 24 hours a day, not only for its propaganda value but also as a way of diverting German fighters from the Russian Front. To this end, No 2 Group staged a series of high-profile daylight raids in addition to its normal fare of shipping strikes and 'Circus' operations. On 4 July, 12 Blenheims launched a daring attack on Bremen, despite the lack of any cloud cover. Four were lost. On 12 August, 54 crews from six squadrons made their deepest penetration yet into *Reich* territory to bomb two major power stations near Cologne, one of which, at Knapsack, is seen in this photograph taken during the attack. A total of ten bombers — almost a fifth of the force — were shot down by flak and fighters. **C 2020**

Right:
The crew of a Blenheim IV of No 88 (Hong Kong) Squadron climb from their aircraft at Attlebridge, Norfolk, after returning from an Army co-operation exercise, 16 August 1941. For a short period in the summer and autumn of 1941, the squadron operated Blenheims on 'Circus' operations over northern France and, flying from Manston, as part of Operation 'Channel Stop', the RAF's costly attempt to close the Channel to German shipping in daylight. That summer the squadron became the first in No 2 Group to take delivery of a batch of the new American-built Douglas Boston IIIs, although these would not become operational for several months. **CH 17172**

Left:
A gunner's view of a trawler burning after being hit during an anti-shipping strike by Blenheims off the Dutch coast on 18 August 1941. In order to assess the results of these attacks, the WOP/AGs were provided with Leica cameras to record any hits achieved. Two ships were sunk on this operation, which benefited from an escort of long-range Spitfires, two of which can be seen in the photograph. As summer gave way to autumn and Blenheim squadrons began to be transferred to the Middle East, No 2 Group's anti-shipping raids were gradually scaled down. Though very costly, they were nevertheless considered a success. **C 2039**

Below:
We can laugh about it now! The rear gunner (left) and pilot of a No 149 Squadron Wellington, safely back at Mildenhall, examine the damage caused to their aircraft by a German night-fighter, possibly during the raid on Kiel, 19/20 August 1941. During the attack, the fabric covering the rear fuselage caught fire, and the rear gunner had to use his parachute pack to beat out the flames. The Wellington's unique geodetic construction enabled it to take such punishment in its stride. **CH 3428**

Above: An interior view of a Manchester of No 207 Squadron, looking aft towards the rear turret with a member of the crew posing by the flare chute, September 1941. The fuselage design was one of the more successful features of the Manchester; it was spacious for the crew and enclosed a capacious, uninterrupted bomb bay. This was due to Avro's design team faithfully adhering to the Air Ministry's specifications of 1936 that the aircraft be able to accommodate two 18in torpedoes. As a result, the aircraft could carry over 10,000lb of bombs including — with slight modifications — the new 4,000lb 'Cookie'. **CH 3884**

Above: Wellington II W5444/EP-K of No 104 Squadron awaits delivery of its load of 250- and 500-pounders at Driffield, autumn 1941. The squadron was one of two Wellington-equipped units to form in No 4 Group in April 1941 (the other was the Canadian No 405 Squadron). It flew a total of 373 sorties with the comparatively rare Merlin-engined Mk II variant from its Yorkshire base before transferring to the Middle East at the end of the year. **HU 75017**

Above: On the night of 7/8 September 1941 Bomber Command broke another grim record — the heaviest losses in one night so far in the war. In a major raid on Berlin and diversionary attacks on Kiel and Boulogne, 18 aircraft out of 295 despatched were lost. This Stirling, N6045/LS-U from No 15 Squadron, was one of them. Hit by flak, it crash-landed near Steenderen in the Netherlands. The object on the wing is the inflated dinghy. In the second half of the year, the loss rate on night operations began to rise alarmingly. The figures provided worrying evidence that the German night-fighter force was becoming increasingly effective. **HU 25889**

Above:
In September 1941 No 44 Squadron, which had been operational with Bomber Command since the first day of the war, had 'Rhodesia' added to its title, in recognition of that country's contributions to the war effort. Also, at least a quarter of the squadron's personnel was Rhodesian in origin.
On 11 and 12 September an official photographer spent time recording activity with the squadron and its Hampdens at Waddington, both on the ground and — as here — in the air, on practice flights. The foreground aircraft, AE257, was lost on an operation to Bremen on 21/22 October. No trace was found of Pilot Officer W. Budd and his crew. **CH 3481**

Left:
A member of the ground crew poses in the narrow 'fighter-type' cockpit of one of the squadron's Hampdens. Note his 'Rhodesia' shoulder title and the bomb tally painted on the fuselage. At this time, the aircraft had carried out five bombing raids and a mine-laying operation — the 'Gardening' sortie being indicated by a detailed painting of a parachute mine. The squadron flew a total of 2,043 Hampden sorties for the loss of 43 aircraft, before converting to Lancasters at the beginning of 1942. **CH 3484**

Above:
Contact starboard-outer! A member of the ground staff signals 'all clear' before the engines of an early-production Halifax II of No 35 Squadron are started at a damp Linton-on-Ouse, October 1941. Other personnel wait ready to remove the wheel chocks. No 35 Squadron was a former training unit that had been reformed in November 1940 to introduce the Halifax into service. The squadron flew its first Halifax operation on 10/11 March 1941, when six aircraft were sent against Le Havre. Tragically, one of the aircraft was shot down on its return by an RAF night-fighter and all but two of the crew killed. **D 6054**

Right:
The cramped interior of another No 35 Squadron Halifax, on the same date. In this view, looking forward into the narrow, deep cockpit area, the back of the flight engineer can be seen at his take-off position on a collapsible seat beside the pilot, with the wireless operator and observer down below. At this stage of the war many British bombers still carried two pilots, but operational experience had shown that the second pilot was little more than a passenger. With the entry into service of the new four-engined bombers in 1941 and 1942, the position was gradually phased out in favour of a new crew member, the flight engineer, whose job was to assist the pilot and monitor the engines and fuel. As a result, the pressure on pilot training was reduced and Bomber Command was able to deploy a larger force of aircraft. **D 6028**

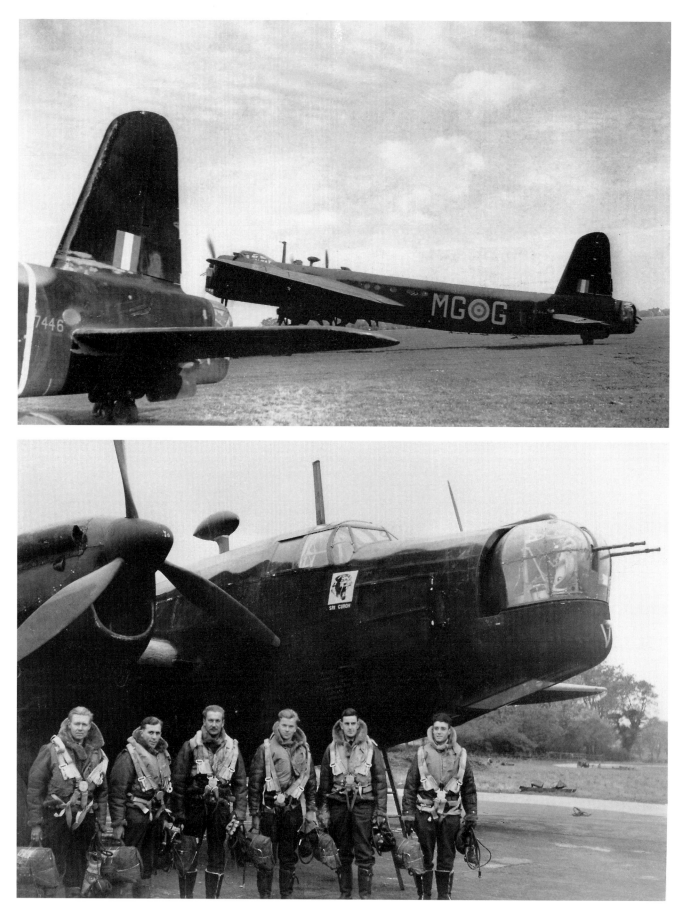

Opposite top:
Stirlings of No 7 Squadron photographed at Oakington on 10 October 1941, during an open day for the Press. The background aircraft, W7444/MG-G, was an early-production model with the rarely-photographed twin-Browning beam guns mounted amidships (just visible behind the wing trailing edge). This design feature was soon changed, and the vast majority of Stirlings were fitted with a mid-upper turret. The aircraft was written-off at the end of the month when its undercarriage collapsed returning from an operational sortie. W7446, its tail visible in the foreground, was another victim of undercarriage failure when it skidded and swung on landing two weeks later. **HU 83510**

Opposite below:
The crew of *Sri Guroh*, a Merlin-engined Wellington II of No 214 (Federated Malay States) Squadron based at Stradishall, Suffolk, photographed in front of their aircraft before setting out for Essen on 4 November 1941. This aircraft, W5442/BU-V, was one of several Wellingtons paid for by funds raised in the Malay States, in accordance with the 'Gift Squadrons' scheme. All were named after towns in Malaya and bore a tiger's head motif. The trip to Essen that night was a small raid, with 28 Wellingtons taking part. All returned safely. **CH 3943**

Above:
A Halifax of No 10 Squadron (previously with No 76 Squadron, judging by the painted-out fuselage codes) is refuelled at Leeming, Yorkshire, on 12 December 1941, soon after the squadron had exchanged its Whitleys for the new four-engined bombers. Almost immediately, the squadron began intensive training for yet another major daylight operation against the *Scharnhorst* and *Gneisenau* at Brest — Operation 'Veracity'. After a number of inconclusive night raids on the harbour, the operation went ahead with 47 Halifaxes, Stirlings and Manchesters attacking on 18 December; daylight was considered essential to ensure a reasonable chance of hitting these pin-point targets. Bombing from 16,000ft, some hits were claimed on the sterns of both vessels but six bombers were shot down, mostly by fighters. On 30 December, in the last raid of the year, 16 Halifaxes tried again to cripple the warships during a second daylight operation, but the results could not be accurately assessed. This time, the defences claimed three of the attackers. **CH 4463**

Above: In November 1941, when this photograph of a Whitley crew preparing for a night sortie was taken, that venerable aircraft was still the most numerous type in No 4 Group, although its time as a front-line aircraft with Bomber Command was nearing an end. In December, No 10 Squadron would be the next in the Group to convert to the new Halifaxes. This particular unidentified crew — all sergeants — starred in a photo story released to the Press depicting their experiences before and after a typical raid. In the first of three shots from this sequence, the crew climb into thick sweaters and Irvin two-piece sheepskin flying suits, an hour before take-off. **CH 4187**

Right:
The ground crew wait patiently as last-minute adjustments are made to the pilot's flying clothing at dispersal. Note the parachutes and map bags slung on the ground, and the thermos flask — an essential item of personal kit for a seven-hour flight in a draughty Whitley. Unfortunately no details are available as to the squadron or location for these shots, but the photographer did note that two members of the crew had each completed 30 operations. **CH 4188**

Left:
Their sortie successfully completed, the crew settle down to the traditional post-operation breakfast of bacon and eggs, and a mountain of bread. There are smiles from this veteran crew, but the mounting losses during this period were causing concern. The autumn of 1941 was a grim time for Bomber Command, culminating in record-breaking losses on the Berlin 'op' of 7/8 November. On that occasion No 4 Group lost 12 bombers, including nine of its Whitleys. **CH 4193**

CHAPTER 4

> *'...March 1942 marks the time from which Bomber Command began decisively to advance towards an ultimate operational efficiency which was astonishing.'*
>
> **(Official History, HMSO, 1961)**

1942 is commonly regarded as the turning point of the war, a tumultuous year when, after a bleak start, fortunes began to swing in favour of the Allies. After Japan's unprovoked attack on the American fleet at Pearl Harbour on 7 December 1941, and Hitler's subsequent declaration of war on the United States, the world's most powerful industrial nation was now firmly committed to the Allied cause, and there could no longer be any doubt as to eventual victory. Britain still had to endure serious setbacks in the battle against the U-boats, in North Africa and especially in the Far East, where her possessions were ignominiously surrendered to the Japanese. Before the year was out, however, Japan's onslaught would be checked, US forces would be arriving in Britain, and the German Army, mired in Russia for another winter, would be about to suffer its most significant defeat at Stalingrad. The Washington War Conference at the beginning of 1942 reaffirmed Allied strategy to tackle Germany first and Japan second, a central tenet of the plan being the wearing down of German war industry by bombing as a prelude to an invasion of continental Europe. These unfolding events, and the evolution of Allied strategy, would have vital implications for Bomber Command.

The Air Staff considered the time was now right for a resumption of Bomber Command's offensive against Germany, following the period of restraint and recuperation over the winter months. On 14 February a new directive was issued to Air Marshal J. E. A. Baldwin, who was acting as 'caretaker' C-in-C following the dismissal of Sir Richard Peirse in January. Peirse had been held responsible for the disastrous raid on Berlin on 7/8 November 1941, and suffered the consequences of being at the helm throughout a period of heavy losses and poor results. The new directive stated that the primary objective of operations should be 'focused on the morale of the enemy civil population and in particular, of the industrial workers'. Great expectations were placed on 'Gee', the new radio navigation aid now entering service, which enabled navigators to obtain a fix of their position using pulsed radio signals emitted from three ground stations in Britain. The Air Staff assured Baldwin that '...the introduction of TR 1335 ['Gee'] will confer upon your forces the ability to concentrate their effort to an extent which has not hitherto been possible under the operational conditions with which you are faced. It is accordingly considered that the introduction of this equipment on operations should be regarded as a revolutionary advance in bombing technique...' The experts considered that 'Gee' would have a life of six months before the enemy came up with successful countermeasures, and so the maximum effort was to be expended in this period to make full use of it.

Four industrial areas of the Ruhr and Rhineland within 'Gee' range (approximately 350-400 miles) were to be the primary targets: Essen, Duisburg, Düsseldorf and Cologne. Three northerly ports — Bremen, Wilhelmshaven and Emden — were listed as secondary targets, and a third group of more distant objectives beyond the range of 'Gee', including Berlin, were to be attacked when weather conditions were favourable. A subsequent minute from the Chief of the Air Staff aimed to clear up any confusion over an annexe to the directive which listed a selection of individual industrial plants suitable for precision attack if accuracy allowed: '...the aiming points are to be built-up areas, *not*, for instance, the dockyards or aircraft factories...' Bomber Command's primary effort was thus to be directed towards breaking the enemy's morale through the deliberate area bombing of industrial cities. The directive represented a culmination of two years of painful experience and experiment, during which a bombing policy had evolved primarily on the grounds of operational feasibility rather than strategic or moral desirability. The area bombing of German cities had emerged by default as Bomber Command's only practicable course of action, one that had been dictated by the force's inability to carry out precision attacks at night. The policy would continue for the rest of the war, even after the techniques for accurate night bombing had been developed, and would be the cause of bitter controversy long afterwards.

The 'Channel Dash' of 12 February, when Bomber Command's old enemies, the *Scharnhorst* and *Gneisenau*, in company with *Prinz Eugen*, made a successful attempt to sail back to Germany under the noses of the Royal Navy, at least rid the RAF of the need to continue its costly raids on Brest, which had occupied much attention over the winter months. Frantic attempts to find and attack the ships failed, but both were slightly damaged off the Frisian Islands by mines laid earlier by Bomber Command aircraft. However, the Admiralty still opposed the build-up of the bomber force, arguing that long-range aircraft could do more good against ships and submarines at sea, both in the Atlantic and elsewhere. Opposition from the Naval Staff was to be expected, but dissent came from other quarters as well. The issue was raised in the House of Commons by Sir Stafford Cripps, Lord Privy Seal, who questioned the continuing use of heavy bombers against Germany. He and other critics claimed that, as a result of the broadening of the war, the strategic bomber offensive no longer represented the sole means to strike at Germany. With other potential avenues of attack now open, and the pressing needs of the forces in other theatres of war, they questioned the wisdom of continuing to

pour huge resources into Bomber Command. The debate stirred up fresh anxieties which threatened the very future of the campaign.

Fortunately for Bomber Command at this moment of crisis, a new Commander-in-Chief was appointed who believed whole-heartedly in the bomber offensive and who was determined to silence its critics. Formerly the head of the permanent RAF delegation in the United States and, before that, AOC of No 5 Group in 1940, Air Marshal Arthur Harris took up his appointment on 22 February and would lead Bomber Command for the rest of the war. A tough, plain-speaking and resolute leader with an unshakeable faith in strategic bombing, Harris was utterly convinced of the war-winning potential of the force now under his command, and had no qualms about following the area bombing policy which he inherited. In the next three years, he would prosecute the offensive against German cities with such single-minded determination — some would say bordering on the obsessional — that it would lead to his abrupt downfall at the end of the war and subsequent castigation. Yet there can be little doubt that Harris's qualities of leadership were inspirational to Bomber Command, especially at this time of uncertainty and wavering convictions. In March he received indirect help in the form of Lord Cherwell, who provided Churchill with a mathematical study of the effects of bombing on German towns. The Prime Minister's scientific adviser confidently predicted that, if half the bomb loads of the 10,000 bombers that Britain should be able to produce before mid-1943 were dropped on the 58 German towns with populations exceeding 100,000 inhabitants, then a third of the entire German population would be rendered homeless. 'There seems little doubt,' Cherwell confidently asserted, 'that this would break the spirit of the people.' Though his methods and conclusions were undoubtedly unsound and overly optimistic, Cherwell's influential intervention in the strategic debate proved decisive. It only remained for Harris to show what Bomber Command could do.

The force which Harris inherited was, however, still far too small for any grand design. Losses, production delays, and the constant drain of other RAF and Coastal Command requirements had kept the number of available aircraft down to a level little improved on that of a year earlier. It was the cause of much exasperation that, of 19 new squadrons formed within Bomber Command in 1942, 13 would be transferred to the Middle East or other Commands. There was also a serious deficiency in trained crews. On the day Harris became C-in-C, Bomber Command's front-line strength totalled 446 serviceable medium and heavy bombers — mostly Wellingtons and Hampdens — and 72 light bombers, the majority of these still Blenheims, augmented by some of the new, superior, American-

Above: A student observer contemplates his 'office' in the nose of a Hampden before embarking on an early-morning flight at No 5 Air Observers School at Jurby on the Isle of Man, January 1942. Previously known as No 5 Bombing & Gunnery School, this was one of many training units which relocated from the east coast of England to safer skies when war broke out. By 1942 the unit was operating a variety of aircraft including Ansons, Blenheims, Hampdens and the unreliable Herefords. The course covered not only air navigation but also bombing and gunnery, all of which the trainee observers of Bomber Command were required to learn. **CH 4864**

built Bostons. Both of the latter types were unsuited to the strategic offensive, but would continue to be used by No 2 Group for minor daylight harassing operations over occupied Europe. There were still less than 100 of the new four-engined 'heavies' in service, and few of the new Lancasters, but production was at last getting into gear; the process of re-equipping the squadrons continued throughout the year, so that the bomb-lifting capacity of the force, if not its numerical strength, increased considerably. After conspicuous service, the venerable Whitleys flew their last operational bombing sorties in April, as No 4 Group continued converting to Halifaxes. The final Hampdens bowed out in September, by which time No 5 Group, after an unhappy period with the ill-fated Manchesters, had become an all-Lancaster force.

Although area attacks on the morale of the German industrial workforce was now the primary objective, Harris's initial operations were against the *Scharnhorst* and *Gneisenau* in the north German ports. A lucky hit on the latter ship at Kiel on the night of 26/27 February succeeded in putting her out of action for the rest of the war. His first major success against a land target was a night precision raid on the Renault vehicle factory at Billancourt, just outside Paris, on 3/4 March. Here the bombers achieved good results, attacking at lower than normal altitudes by the light of flares dropped by 'raid leaders', and achieving a record degree of concentration of 121 aircraft an hour over the factory. With 'Gee' finally ready for service, the assault on Germany's industrial heart could not be delayed and a series of raids against Essen were planned. The first of these occurred on 8/9 March, with the leading 'Gee'-equipped aircraft dropping flares and incendiaries to illuminate and mark the target for the rest of the force carrying high-explosive loads. This was known as the 'Shaker' technique and was used in eight major attacks against Essen in March and April, but with disappointing results. Rather more success was achieved with a 'Gee'-led raid on Cologne on 13/14 March, which saw accurate bombing and significant damage inflicted on industrial plants and rail yards.

The Air Ministry directive had stressed the importance of using fire-raising weapons, which would not only increase the amount of destruction inflicted on a target but also usefully illuminate the relevant aiming points. In accordance with this, on the night of 28/29 March Harris chose to attack the Baltic port of Lübeck to test the theory of saturation incendiary tactics. Lübeck was beyond 'Gee' range, but the device enabled those bombers fitted with it to navigate part of the way. Flares and incendiaries dropped by the leading aircraft once again illuminated the target for following crews, who were also helped by the town's coastline location and a bright moonlit night. The results of the raid were dramatic. Almost half of the town, sub-sequently described by Harris as 'built more like a fire-lighter than a human habitation', was consumed in the conflagration. A similar level of destruction was wrought on Rostock, further along the Baltic coast, during four raids at the end of April. Unfortunately, Bomber Command was unable to replicate these successes over the Ruhr, with raids there continuing to produce

disappointing results. Locating a target was a relatively straight-forward task at low altitude over a lightly defended coastline objective, but an altogether tougher proposition over the heart of the Ruhr, with its dazzling searchlights, decoy fires and strong flak defences.

To quell any remaining doubts as to the potential of Bomber Command, Harris secured approval from Portal and Churchill to despatch a force of 1,000 bombers in a concentrated attack against a major German target. With a normally available front-line force of less than 500 aircraft, Operation 'Millennium' would require the heavy conversion and operational training units to contribute aircraft, to be flown by instructors and advanced pupils. Coastal Command also agreed to lend squadrons for the assault, but at the last minute the Admiralty vetoed their use. Harris was forced to make up the shortfall from his own resources, which meant scraping together every last reserve aircraft, and making even more extensive use of trainee crews. In the event, virtually every aircraft in Bomber Command was committed and an armada of 1,047 bombers readied for a moonlit assault on Hamburg. After several postponements due to bad weather, Harris switched to the secondary target of Cologne and on 30/31 May achieved a spectacular success over that unfortunate city. The raid employed tactics of concentration in time and space which became routine in later Bomber Command operations; all aircraft were sent at various altitudes along the same route to form a 'bomber stream', so that as few as possible were exposed to night-fighter interception as they penetrated the belt of enemy radar defences. Similar concentration over the target was intended to overwhelm the city's defences and inflict the maximum amount of damage, and in this Bomber Command was extremely successful; 1,455 tons of bombs were dropped — of which two-thirds were incendiaries — in an attack of 90 minutes' duration, which devastated 600 acres, and 'de-housed' over 45,000 people. Once again, 'Gee'-equipped raid leaders used flares to guide following aircraft. Fears that many aircraft would be lost in collisions over the target proved unfounded, but 41 aircraft still failed to return — a new record for a Bomber Command operation.

Harris sought to make full use of his painfully acquired force, and so two nights later a follow-up 'Thousand Bomber' raid was carried out against Essen, though with far less success. This time, slightly fewer than 1,000 aircraft were despatched, but the bombing was widely scattered as a result of cloud and haze obscuring the target. The third and last 'Thousand' raid was delivered against Bremen on 25/26 June. Once again, cloud prevented accurate bombing, although the results achieved were far better than the previous Essen operation. Bomber Command casualties were the heaviest of the three raids; 50 aircraft were lost, including an alarming 33 crews from the training units. Such a wastage of instructors and advanced pupils could not be tolerated; henceforth the OTUs and conversion units would rarely be called upon to supplement the main force on operations. By committing the entire force, and depleting the reserves and the training organisation, these big raids had been a risky venture; because of this they were never repeated. It would not be until 1944 that a greatly expanded Bomber Command was able to despatch a similar number of aircraft against a single objective. However, despite the losses, Harris had achieved a major success and a great morale boost for the country as a whole. It was a portent of the level of destruction which Bomber Command might achieve on a regular basis if given the necessary resources. Operationally, the tactics of the bomber stream and concentration over the target were seen as vital to future success. However, the problem remained of establishing a reliable method of identifying and marking the target in all weather conditions, and in the face of vigorous German resistance.

This problem may have been a factor in Harris's decision to despatch formations of his recently delivered Lancasters on precision daylight and dusk attacks on a number of occasions during 1942. On 17 April, 12 Lancasters from Nos 44 and 97 Squadrons were despatched on a low-level operation against the MAN submarine diesel engine factory at Augsburg. Despite various diversionary operations over northern France, seven aircraft were shot down. The raid leader, Squadron Leader J. D. Nettleton of No 44 Squadron, limped home in a badly shot-up aircraft to be awarded the Victoria Cross. Further, less costly, daylight raids took place later in the year: on 11 July, 44 Lancasters made a 1,500-mile round trip to the submarine yards at Danzig which, due to a circuitous route mostly over water and much of it in darkness, resulted in only two aircraft being shot down; and an attack by 94 aircraft on the Schneider armaments factory at Le Creusot in France — Operation 'Robinson' —occurred on 17 October. These experimental raids, though daring and courageously executed, proved only that daylight attacks were no more feasible when carried out by Lancasters than they were when less well regarded types were involved. The problem, of course, was one of tactics, not aircraft design. Daylight incursions on a smaller scale continued sporadically for much of the spring and summer, specifically 'Moling' or 'Scuttle' sorties by individual or small groups of bombers using heavy cloud cover to mask their approach. Many of these harassing raids were abandoned prematurely due to clearing skies before the targets could be identified and bombed.

If such raids proved to be inefficient and wasteful affairs, operations carried out by No 2 Group, the daylight specialists, were even more hazardous, and similarly of little relevance to the main strategic offensive. Using a variety of aircraft types, the group maintained its varied fare of 'Circus' operations, intruder sorties and precision attacks on targets in the occupied countries. By the autumn the last of the valiant Blenheims had been withdrawn, and apart from two Mosquito squadrons, the other units were flying the popular Boston or converting to two other American-built types about to enter service, the not-so-popular Ventura and the Mitchell medium bomber. A major raid by all of the group's squadrons on the Philips works at Eindhoven in December was a great success, but, like many operations by the day bomber force when carried out beyond the limited range of escorting fighters, it resulted in a prohibitive number of casualties. Even the new Mosquito bombers, relying on speed alone to evade interception, suffered surprisingly high losses in their early operations against German targets.

In the meantime, Bomber Command needed to find ways of improving its bombing accuracy at night. Although much heralded, 'Gee' had been something of a disappointment. It was considered a useful navigational tool, but was not accurate enough to use for blind-bombing; by August it had, as predicted, been severely disrupted over enemy territory by jamming. Bomber Command remained essentially a 'fair weather' force, still dependent on visual identification of its objectives, which was often very difficult or impossible over the Ruhr targets. As a consequence, the majority of bombs dropped were still going astray, even missing entirely the towns and cities in which the chosen targets lay. The problem continued to exercise the minds of airmen and 'boffins' alike. New technological devices were on their way, but for now many in Bomber Command believed that the best way forward was to develop the earlier technique of raid leaders by creating a special target-finding force of experienced crews who could identify and mark aiming points for the main body following behind. The champion of these ideas at the Air Ministry was the Deputy Director of Bomber Operations, Group Captain Syd Bufton, a former operational squadron commander, who put forward the idea of a separate, specialised force of six squadrons to carry out this task for the rest of the Command.

Unfortunately, Bufton's proposals met with hostility from Harris and his group commanders, who preferred the idea of natural competition within the squadrons to improve efficiency rather than the creation of an elite organisation. Nevertheless, after prolonged debate the Chief of the Air Staff was convinced of the plan and ordered Harris to establish what became known as the Pathfinder Force (PFF). The Pathfinders would be commanded by a noted Australian-born pilot and navigation expert with recent operational experience, Air Commodore Donald Bennett, and consisted initially of one squadron taken from each of the main force groups. On 18/19 August, the new force flew its first operation when it attempted — unsuccessfully in the event — to mark Flensburg on the Baltic coast. Indeed, early PFF operations brought little overall improvement in Bomber Command results, due to a lack of accurate bombing aids or effective means to mark the target. However, by the use of illuminating flares dropped by the lead aircraft, backed up by such expedients as coloured marker flares and incendiary bombs, the Pathfinders were able to bring about a significant increase in bombing concentration, even if they could do little to improve bombing accuracy. Fortunately, the new force was about to be provided with a significant new blind-bombing aid called 'Oboe'. With this device, which underwent operational trials in PFF Mosquitos in December, and the advent of new purpose-designed target indicator bombs, Harris's crews would, at last, have the ability to mark and bomb accurately, irrespective of the cloud, industrial haze or searchlight glare that they so often encountered.

Bomber Command was not alone in benefiting from advances in technology; German scientists were rendering the night skies less safe for the bombers. As 1942 progressed, RAF losses due to radar-equipped night-fighters increased. The German air defence network was based on a chain of radar 'boxes' — areas of sky in which fighters could be vectored by ground controllers onto individual bombers passing through on their way to their targets. Many Luftwaffe fighters now had radar sets of their own which gave them a greatly increased chance of a successful interception. Radar-directed flak and searchlight defences had also been massively strengthened and were now concentrated around the key targets, especially in the Ruhr. Bomber Command was still too small to saturate the defences on normal operations and was still obliged to carry out major attacks in moonlight conditions, which now only favoured the defenders. The German defences caused losses to rise from 2.5% at the beginning of the year to over double that figure by the late autumn. The Stirlings of No 3 Group and the Halifax squadrons of No 4 Group were suffering even higher casualty rates as they struggled with aircraft plagued by design flaws or technical problems. Such losses were unsustainable in the long run and made more urgent the development of radio countermeasures. One of the first of these, codenamed 'Shiver', was aimed at the flak and fighter control Würzburg radar frequencies and was ready in October. It would be followed by a plethora of ground and airborne devices intended to jam, or otherwise disrupt, the enemy's ability to 'see' and communicate in the night skies over Germany.

After a year of struggling to maintain its strength and overcome major obstacles to finding and hitting its targets, Bomber Command was now at last on the threshold of a period of massive expansion and operational success. Harris described 1942 as the 'preliminary phase', a year of preparation, consolidation and experiment. At the end of it, little real harm had been done to the enemy, but the fundamental tactics of night area bombing had been developed. Crucially, the bomber force had received, or was about to receive, a host of new navigation, blind-bombing and target-marking devices which would initiate, as Harris put it, 'a new era in the technique of night bombing' and enable what he described later as the 'main offensive' to begin. In this endeavour Bomber Command would be joined by a new ally. In August the US Eighth Air Force had begun flying operational missions from Britain against targets in enemy-occupied Europe, and, despite concerns voiced by its British counterpart, would in the new year extend its daylight precision attacks into the heart of the *Reich* itself. From now on, the strategic bombing offensive against Germany would take place by day and night. The 'Whirlwind' was about to begin.

Above:

A Stirling crew of No 7 Squadron are interrogated on their return from the raid on the Renault factory at Billancourt in Paris, 3/4 March 1942. In the largest Bomber Command operation yet despatched against a single target, 235 aircraft carried out an especially concentrated attack, illuminating the target with flares and dropping a record tonnage of bombs. They achieved considerable success, destroying a significant portion of the plant and putting back lorry production by several months. Only one aircraft — a Wellington — was lost, but several hundred French workers, who ignored the sirens, died in the attack. **CH 5126**

Left:

A Boston III undergoing an overhaul at an unidentified maintenance unit, March 1942. Note the serial number, W8271, on the open roof hatch. This aircraft served with No 88 Squadron at Attlebridge, one of three squadrons in No 2 Group that operated the type during 1942. It was later transferred to No 418 Squadron, Fighter Command, for use in the intruder role. Bostons first saw action with Bomber Command on 12 February 1942 — before they were officially declared operational — during the so-called 'Channel Dash'. In March they were committed to the daylight offensive, taking part in 'Circus' operations and raids on power stations and harbour installations in northern France. A sturdy and manoeuvrable aircraft, the Boston was well regarded, being faster than a Blenheim and with a greater bomb capacity. Its fixed forward-firing armament of four .303in Browning machine guns also gave it a useful punch on low-level operations. **E(MoS) 713**

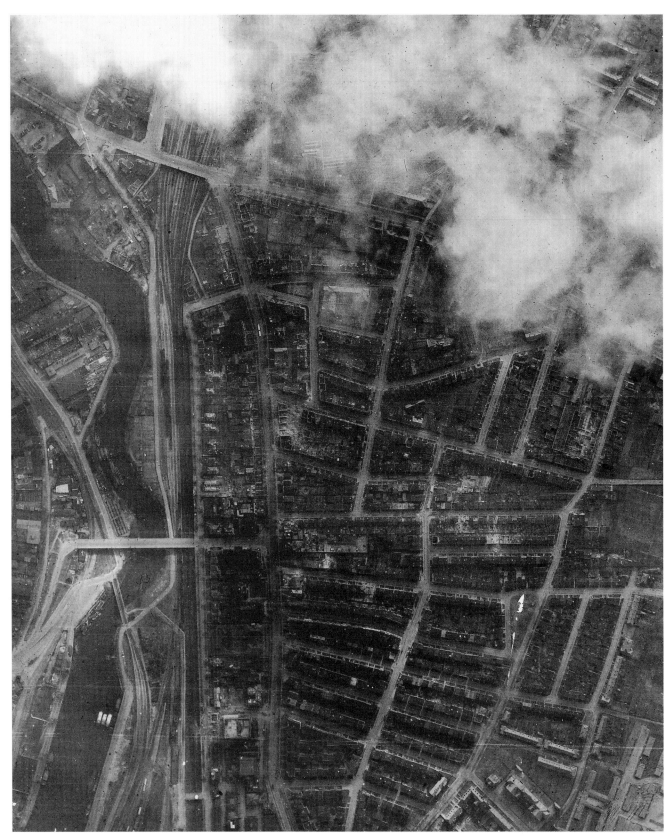

Above: When Air Marshal Arthur Harris became Commander-in-Chief of Bomber Command on 22 February 1942, he inherited a policy of area bombing which had evolved as a result of the failure of night precision attacks. The raid on Lübeck on the Baltic Coast on the night of 28/29 March was his first dramatic success in accordance with that policy. In a concentrated attack, 234 bombers dropped their predominantly incendiary loads onto the densely packed streets in the heart of the city, burning out some 200 acres, part of which can be seen in this reconnaissance photo taken on the morning after the raid. 320 Germans died, the highest casualty total so far for a single raid on a German town, and 12 RAF aircraft were lost. The strategic offensive had been elevated to a new level of destruction. **C 2388**

Right:
Two Bostons over Le Havre docks during a daylight raid by 12 aircraft of No 226 Squadron on 16 April 1942. Bombs can be seen exploding across the basins and quays below. A nearby power station was also attacked. The following day Nos 88 and 107 Squadron Bostons, accompanied by a massive fighter escort, raided targets in Rouen and Calais as part of the diversionary effort set up for the famous Lancaster raid on Augsburg. **C 2386**

Above: A typical group of 'Aussie' aircrew of No 460 Squadron, RAAF, photographed on 21 April 1942. The squadron formed in November 1941 and began operations with No 1 Group at Breighton, Yorkshire, in March 1942, flying Wellingtons. In 50 bombing, nine mine-laying and two leaflet-dropping raids, No 460 Squadron lost 29 Wellingtons — the highest percentage loss of all Bomber Command Wellington units. In October, the squadron re-equipped with Lancasters. **CH 5354**

Left:
Bombing-up a Stirling of No 1651 Heavy Conversion Unit (HCU) on a bright spring day at Waterbeach, Cambridgeshire, 30 April 1942. HCUs were formed within each group to provide crews from the operational training units with a second stage of advanced training on the more complex four-engined aircraft that were now equipping the squadrons in ever greater numbers. In 1942 the training units provided aircraft with mixed crews of instructors and pupils for the 'Thousand Bomber' raids and other 'maximum effort' operations. In 73 sorties flown by Stirling conversion units, mostly in 1942, five aircraft were lost. **CH 5474**

Below:
Winston Churchill, in the uniform of an Air Commodore, with Dr E. H. Evatt (Australian Minister for External Affairs), Clement Attlee (Deputy Prime Minister) and Air Vice-Marshal C. R. Carr (AOC No 4 Group) during a visit to a Yorkshire-based Halifax squadron in May 1942. While there, and without prior warning, the Prime Minister requested that an anti-invasion drill be carried out and watched as everyone from cooks to aircrew grabbed rifles and took up defensive positions. **CH 5460**

Right:
Air Marshal A. T. Harris (later Air Chief Marshal Sir Arthur), Air Officer Commanding-in-Chief, Bomber Command, at work in his office at Command Headquarters at Naphill, near High Wycombe, May 1942. With him are his senior officers, Air Vice-Marshals R. Graham (left) and R. Saundby. Saundby was Bomber Command SASO (Senior Air Staff Officer) and later Deputy AOC-in-C. A keen fisherman, it was he who decided on the names of fish as codewords for Bomber Command targets. Thus Berlin became 'Whitebait', Bremen 'Salmon' and Cologne 'Trout'. **CH 5492**

Below:
Wing Commander Guy Gibson DFC and Bar (centre, with moustache), the CO of No 106 Squadron, with members of his squadron at Coningsby on 31 May 1942, after the 'Thousand Bomber' raid to Cologne. Note the Manchesters parked in the background. The squadron started converting to Lancasters in May, with the Manchesters flying their last 'ops' in June. With his fame leading No 617 Squadron still in the future, Gibson took over No 106 in April and quietly moulded it into the premier squadron in No 5 Group. This was shown by the squadron's low loss and abort rates, the high number of aircraft available for operations, and its top position in the group's bombing results ladder. **ZZZ 6965C**

Above: A Wellington under construction at the Vickers 'Shadow factory' at Hawarden, near Chester, 1 June 1942. The 'Shadow' scheme, first proposed in 1935, was designed to ensure the quantity production of aircraft and aero-engines in dispersed Government-owned factories in the North and Midlands, easing pressure on the parent companies and enabling them to concentrate on research and development. The two Vickers shadow factories at Chester and Blackpool turned out four times the number of aircraft built by the original plant at Weybridge. Chester did not have any manufacturing capability of its own; it was simply a huge mass-production assembly plant, with all components coming in from some 500 outside sub-contractors. Almost 70% of its final assembly workers were women. In total, 11,460 Wellingtons were produced at the three locations, more than any other type of British bomber. The last example was handed over to the RAF in October 1945. **CH 5987**

Left:
This early production Halifax II Series I, in a photograph released in June 1942, was a development aircraft operated by Handley Page. By this date, the deterioration in the performance of the Halifax II was giving concern. Additions to the aircraft's airframe and internal equipment had increased weight and drag, while engine power had remained static. The bulky Boulton Paul C Mk II mid-upper turret, introduced with this variant, is shown to advantage. Other detrimental changes introduced in early 1942 included the fitting of large asbestos exhaust shrouds, which caused airflow problems over the wings, and the application of 'Special Night' black paint, the texture of which was rough enough to reduce airspeed. Some squadrons had already started the process of cleaning up the aircraft by removing various fittings and taking off the new turret. However, the most critical and persistent problem affecting the Halifax, which had led to a series of unexplained crashes, was that of rudder overbalance. Under certain conditions, especially when both port engines were feathered, airflow turbulence over the triangular tail-fins caused the rudders to lock hard over, inducing a fatal spin. With modifications, the problem was ameliorated, but never completely overcome until new larger, rectangular 'D' fins were introduced in 1943. **E(MoS) 790**

Right:
In the summer of 1942 Bomber Command received another new US-built aircraft type, the North American Mitchell, to be used in the day bomber role by No 2 Group. A small number of B-25B Mitchell Is were delivered in May and June, of which this aircraft, FK161, was the first. These were mainly used for training, and it was not until September that initial deliveries of the main operational version, the B-25C Mitchell II, were made to Nos 98 and 180 Squadrons at West Raynham. A host of technical problems, however, delayed their combat debut until January 1943. **MH 5773**

Below:
Another Lancaster from No 83 Squadron, this time R5610/OL-G. This aircraft flew its first operational sortie on the famous Cologne raid on 30/31 May. It went on to complete 18 operational flights, including several mine-laying sorties, before being lost on a trip to Frankfurt on 24/25 August. No 83 Squadron was chosen as one of the original squadrons of the Pathfinder Force, set up on 15 August 1942 to help find and mark targets for the Main Force. **CH 6061**

Above:
An Avro Lancaster I, R5852/OL-Y, of No 83 Squadron, June 1942. Its original, overpainted No 44 Squadron codes, 'EM-R', are just visible. Avro's Chief Designer, Roy Chadwick, first conceived the idea of a Manchester powered by four Merlin engines in 1939, long before the original Rolls-Royce Vulture-powered version had even entered production. The quiet gestation of the new design coincided with Air Ministry plans to equip Bomber Command with a four-engined force, and the new aircraft showed such promise that in late 1940 a prototype, dubbed Manchester III, was ordered. This flew in January 1941 and, soon after, a production contract was issued for the aircraft, now christened Lancaster. On Christmas Eve 1941, No 44 Squadron took delivery of the first 'Lancs', by which time the decision had been taken to concentrate on maximum production of the new bomber. By June 1942, seven squadrons were equipped, and Bomber Command at last had a suitable weapon with which to carry out its main offensive. **CH 6071**

Above:
On 27/28 June 1942 144 aircraft of Bomber Command visited Bremen again, only two nights after the city had endured the third of the famous 'Thousand Bomber' raids. Further damage was inflicted, and another nine RAF aircraft were shot down. Stirling N3751/BU-P of No 214 Squadron just managed to make it back after an eventful flight. Damaged by flak, the aircraft also survived repeated enemy fighter attacks during which the rear gunner was killed. Sergeant F. M. Griggs, RAAF, eventually brought the Stirling in for a successful wheels-up landing at Stradishall. **CH 17360**

Opposite:
Sergeant Frank Griggs points to some of the more minor damage to his aircraft. In recognition of their determination and bravery in fighting off their attackers and getting their aircraft home, Griggs and the surviving members of his crew were all awarded the Distinguished Flying Medal. Frank Griggs and his navigator, Sergeant 'Pat' O'Hara (extreme right), went on to serve together with No 109 Squadron, flying 'Oboe' Mosquitos. **CH 17359**

Above: A Stirling of No 218 Squadron towers over a bomb tractor with its train of incendiaries at Marham, June 1942. The main incendiary weapon of Bomber Command was the 4lb magnesium bomb, carried in tin boxes called 'small bomb containers' (SBCs) which remained in the aircraft once the bombs had been released. Their main shortcoming was that they were impossible to aim accurately, and could prove hazardous to other aircraft below. Nevertheless, vast numbers of them were used by Bomber Command and, when used in conjunction with high-capacity blast-bombs ('Cookies'), proved to be the most effective weapon for destroying large city areas. **CH 6278**

Above:

On 29 July 1942 the Duke of Kent visited Mildenhall, home to No 419 Squadron, RCAF, which had participated in major raids against Hamburg on the previous two nights. On both occasions Bomber Command suffered heavily; 59 aircraft failed to return from the two operations, including No 419's CO, Wing Commander John Fulton. 'Moose' Fulton had commanded the squadron since its formation in December 1941 and, to commemorate him, his nickname would be added to the squadron's title. The Duke of Kent (centre, facing camera), seen here exchanging words with some of the Canadians, was himself tragically killed in an air crash in Scotland only a month after this photograph was taken. **CH 6386**

Right:

In August 1942 Lancaster I R5727 became the first of its type to fly the Atlantic, having been chosen as the pattern machine for production of the Lancaster in Canada. It is seen here at Prestwick airport before the flight. Of interest is the rarely seen Nash & Thompson FN64 ventral gun turret, which proved unwieldy and was usually removed from aircraft in Nos 1 and 5 Groups, although some squadrons experimented with other forms of ventral armament. Victory Aircraft Ltd at Malton, Ontario, eventually produced 430 Lancaster Mk Xs, the first deliveries of which began in September 1943. **CH 6701**

Left:
The Armaments Officer at Waterbeach, Pilot Officer J. Whellens (right), on his rounds in the armoury inspecting his staff at work loading belts of .303in ammunition, August 1942. His was just one of many ground jobs, carried out by officers as well as non-commissioned ranks, that the Air Ministry was keen to bring to the public's attention, in order to demonstrate the complexity of the organisation that sent the heavy bombers into the air, and to counter the idea that raids could be mounted at the drop of a hat. Waterbeach was home at this time to the Stirlings of No 1651 Heavy Conversion Unit. **CH 6543**

Right:
Another key ground task was that of Flying Control Officer, in this case Pilot Officer R. P. Burrows, seen here with a WAAF radio-telephone operator in the control room at Linton-on-Ouse, August 1942. Nearing base, a bomber pilot has requested a barometer reading so that his aircraft's altimeter can be set before landing. The blackboard in front of the WAAF operator appears to show three aircraft, 'M', 'J' and 'X', at various altitudes in the landing circuit. **CH 6588**

Above:
Two photographs showing a Stirling I of No 218 (Gold Coast) Squadron being bombed-up at Downham Market, Norfolk, in the summer of 1942, soon after the airfield, which was a satellite of Marham, opened. The bomb train has arrived at the Stirling's dispersal and a pair of 1,000lb GP bombs is about to be pushed into position beneath the aircraft. Note the hoist cables from the bomb winches hanging down through the bomb bay, and the 'trolley-ac' (trolley accumulator) beneath the fuselage, supplying power to the Stirling's electrical systems. Grassy airfield dispersals, which were common in the early years of the war, might be firm enough during a dry summer, but when rain-soaked were totally unsuitable for heavy bombers. **D 8972**

Right:
A sergeant armourer checks a 1,000lb GP bomb before it is winched, by hand, into the Stirling's bomb bay. Note the bomb carrier which contained the electrical release mechanism. The Stirling could carry a maximum load of 14,000lb, but its bomb bay consisted of three narrow parallel cells, each further divided into smaller compartments. Unfortunately, this design imposed a limit on the maximum size bomb that could be carried. The largest was the 2,000lb SAP (semi-armour-piercing) bomb which had been used in 1941 against the German warships at Brest. However, for attacks against industrial cities in Germany, the Stirling's inability to carry a 4,000lb 'Cookie' severely limited its usefulness. **D 8977**

Right:
A photograph worth a thousand words: it is the early hours of the morning at RAF Pocklington, Yorkshire, in late July/early August 1942, and this young Halifax pilot of No 405 (Vancouver) Squadron, RCAF, has just returned from an operation over Germany. No 4 Group was going through a difficult period; a fall-off in the performance of its Halifax IIs was resulting in heavy losses through enemy action and accidents. A total of 109 aircraft had been lost between March and August from 1,770 sorties, representing a loss rate of 6.2%. In August it rose to over 10%. In response, operations were curtailed for a month as the aircraft underwent a programme of 'stop-gap' modifications, which largely consisted of cleaning up the airframe and removing unnecessary equipment to reduce weight and drag.
CH 6627

Left:
The ground staff had their own pressures: engine fitters at Pocklington work quickly to prepare a brand new Rolls-Royce Merlin XX for a waiting Halifax. The 1,280hp Merlin XX engine (which also powered the Lancaster I) was a 12-cylinder in-line liquid-cooled supercharged unit. Four of them could power a Halifax to a maximum speed of about 260mph at 17,000ft, although cruising speed with a normal bomb load was around 200mph. Despite improvements, the Merlin-engined Halifaxes were always considered underpowered, which made the aircraft increasingly vulnerable.
CH 6600

Above:
The CO of No 207 Squadron, Wing Commander F. R. Jeffs DFC , jokes with his Lancaster crews before they set out for a raid, possibly to Düsseldorf on 10 September 1942. No 207 was based at Bottesford, Leicestershire, until 20 September, when it moved to Langar in Nottinghamshire. To counter the freezing conditions in their turrets, the air gunners in the group are equipped with electrically-heated 'Taylorsuits' (which were padded with kapok for buoyancy in water), heated inner gloves and 1940 pattern sheepskin boots. The boots were intended to allow for bulky flying suits to be tucked into them and of necessity were a loose fit, but a major disadvantage was that they could be sucked off in the slipstream if the wearer was unfortunate enough to have to bale out. **CH 7127**

Above: The Bremen raid of 13/14 September 1942 was a 'maximum effort', with 446 bombers taking part, including some from the OTUs. It was the latest in a series of attacks on the port during the summer and early autumn. Further damage was inflicted on industrial premises and the important Focke-Wulf aircraft factory. Of the 21 aircraft lost that night, 17 were Wellingtons, including this one shot down by flak over the Netherlands. With the fabric covering burnt off the fuselage and flying surfaces, the Wellington's famous geodetic airframe structure, designed by Barnes Wallis, is revealed. **HU 8568**

Right:
The entry into operational service of the superlative de Havilland Mosquito bomber was one of the most significant events for Bomber Command in 1942. No 105 Squadron was the first unit to receive the revolutionary aircraft, famously known as the 'Wooden Wonder', and carried out the type's debut combat operation with a high-level 'recce' and bombing sortie against Cologne on 31 May, the morning after the RAF's first 'Thousand' raid. However, it was in daring, low-level daylight and dusk precision attacks that the Mosquito quickly made a name for itself, such as the operation against Gestapo headquarters in Oslo on 25 September 1942, after which the aircraft's existence was revealed to the public. Mosquito IV DK338, seen here displaying its undersurfaces on a test flight in September 1942, would become one of the most successful aircraft in No 105 Squadron, completing 26 'ops' as 'O-Orange' between 12 September 1942 and 1 May 1943, when it crashed soon after take-off at Marham. **CH 7778**

Above: American aircraft production representatives during a tour of the English Electric factory at Preston in the autumn of 1942. At that time English Electric was one of the manufacturing group of companies, with Handley Page at its head, committed to the production of the Halifax, an example of which stands in the background. This aircraft, Halifax II DT567, was destined to be lost on a mine-laying sortie while operating with No 51 Squadron on 8 March 1943. **E(MoS) 933**

Above: A Lancaster I, R5740/KM-O of No 44 Squadron, runs up its engines at Waddington on 12 October 1942. This aircraft was a veteran of Bomber Command operations during the latter part of 1942, taking part in the Le Creusot raid, three trips to Genoa, two to Turin and others to Munich, Hamburg, Kiel and the Ruhr. It was eventually shot down on 25/26 June 1943 while on its 29th operation. **CH 7491**

Above: Lancasters low over the French countryside on their way to the Schneider armament works at Le Creusot, 150 miles southeast of Paris, on 17 October 1942. This is a still from a cine film, made from the aircraft of Wing Commander Guy Gibson by his navigator, Pilot Officer Frank Ruskell. Despite the losses suffered during the famous Augsburg raid in April, Harris elected to send another Lancaster force in daylight against this important target. Ninety-four Lancasters of No 5 Group were despatched on the raid, which was again timed so that the return flight would be made under the cover of darkness. This time, no opposition was encountered and only one aircraft was lost, probably caught in the blast of its own bombs during a subsidiary attack on a nearby electricity transformer at Montchanin. Unfortunately, much of the bombing at Le Creusot fell short, inflicting most damage on French workers' housing nearby, and damage to the factory itself was slight. **C 3183**

Above:
On 22/23 October 1942 Bomber Command renewed its attacks on Italian targets with an operation to Genoa, to coincide with the beginning of Field Marshal Montgomery's offensive at El Alamein. These crews of No 106 Squadron were photographed at rainy Syerston, Nottinghamshire, on the morning after the raid. Fourth from right is Pilot Officer David Shannon, a future 'Dambuster' and leading light of No 617 Squadron. Before the year was out, Bomber Command launched 14 further attacks against Genoa, Milan and Turin as part of a concerted effort to undermine Italian morale. Although the targets were far less heavily defended than those in Germany, the lengthy flights and climb over the Alps took their toll, and were especially hard for the Stirlings with their inferior altitude performance. **CH 17504**

Left:
Squadron Leader The Reverend E. T. Killick (second from right), Station Chaplain at Oakington, hands out 'winter warmers' from the RAF Comforts Fund to ground crew on a crisp autumnal morning, 24 October 1942. Two No 7 Squadron Stirlings loom in the background. RAF padres had a varied role, caring not only for the spiritual and personal welfare of the men and women on the station, but also helping with other activities such as organising entertainments and sporting fixtures. As a former batsman for Cambridge University and Middlesex, as well as a keen rugger player, Reverend Killick was certainly well qualified for the latter. **CH 8741**

Left:
Mosquito IV DK336/GB-P of No 105 Squadron being prepared for a sortie at Marham, late 1942. It was at first unclear what role the Mosquito should play in Bomber Command operations, and early daylight high-level sorties suffered casualties from interceptions by Focke-Wulf FW190s. However, under the inspired leadership of Wing Commander Hughie Edwards VC, who became CO in August and was already a legend in No 2 Group, No 105 Squadron pioneered successful new low-level and shallow diving tactics which involved bombing at dusk and escaping under the cover of darkness. DK336 lasted until 27 January 1943 when it was 'borrowed' by No 139 Squadron, the second Mosquito squadron to form, and crashed in Norfolk returning from the raid on the Burmeister Wain diesel engine plant in Copenhagen. **C 3298**

Above: Flight Sergeant A. M. Halkett DFM (third from right) and his crew pose by the tail of Stirling I N3669/LS-H of No 15 Squadron, after completing the aircraft's 62nd operation, November 1942. It was uncommon for Stirlings to reach such a high score of successful sorties and such an occurrence provided a welcome morale-boosting opportunity, especially at a time when Bomber Command's average loss rate had reached an unsustainable 4.6%. It was recognised that attrition on this scale would ultimately result in a decline of the force, since insufficient crews would survive their first tour of operations to provide the experience and leadership for the new intakes. **CH 7746**

Above:
Wellington IV Z1248 of No 305 (Ziemia Wielkopolska) Squadron, photographed during a visit to No 7 Elementary Flying Training School at Desford, Leicestershire, in late November 1942. No 305 was the fourth and last Polish squadron to form in Bomber Command, beginning operations with No 1 Group in April 1941. This crew had dropped in from their base at Hemswell, Lincolnshire, to provide the trainees with a guided tour of their aircraft, and in so doing gave the photographer an opportunity to set up this comparison shot with one of the school's Tiger Moths. The squadron was one of the few units to be equipped with the rare Wellington IV, which was powered by American Pratt & Whitney Twin Wasps as an insurance against possible shortages of home-grown engines. No 305 would leave Bomber Command in September 1943, re-equipping with Mitchells and operating with the Second Tactical Air Force. **CH 7936**

Left:
Flight Sergeant Leslie Hyder of No 149 Squadron in safe hands while recovering from wounds received over Turin on the night of 28/29 November 1942. Hyder was second pilot in a Stirling which was hit by flak over the target, temporarily rendering the skipper, Flight Sergeant R. H. Middleton, unconscious and sending the aircraft into a dive. Although also wounded, Hyder managed to regain control of the aircraft which went on to release its bombs on the FIAT works. When Middleton regained consciousness, he resumed command despite dreadful head injuries, and nursed his crippled Stirling back over the Alps. Over the English coast he ordered his crew to bale out, but in his weakened state was unable to follow and died with two of his crew as the Stirling crashed into the sea. The four survivors were all decorated; their skipper was awarded a posthumous Victoria Cross. **CH 8167**

Right:
Lockheed Venturas and aircrew of No 464 Squadron, RAAF, at Feltwell, December 1942. The so-called 'Flying Pig' was the least successful of the American-built types used by No 2 Group, suffering from poor handling characteristics and a short range. In the spring of 1942 No 21 Squadron had the dubious honour of being first to equip with the type, followed by No 487 Squadron, RNZAF, in the autumn. Initially intended to replace Blenheims in the night intruder role, the Venturas were instead used on daylight 'Circuses' and low-level cloud cover operations, the first being on 3 November when three aircraft of No 21 Squadron attacked Hengelo in the Netherlands. No 464 Squadron was the third and last squadron to receive Venturas, flying their first operation on the famous Eindhoven raid of 6 December. **CH 8261**

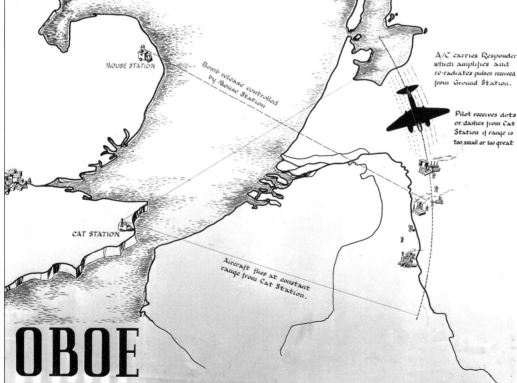

Above: An official illustration explaining the principles of the blind-bombing radar aid 'Oboe', which was used operationally for the first time by three Mosquitos of No 109 Squadron against a power station at Lutterade in the Netherlands on 20/21 December 1942. Two ground stations in England, codenamed 'Cat' and 'Mouse', transmitted audible radio pulses to keep an aircraft on an arc which would bring it over the target, and then signalled the correct moment for its bombs to be released. When used correctly, the device ensured a bombing accuracy within hundreds of yards. However, only six aircraft an hour could be controlled by the system, and its range was limited by the curvature of the earth to about 280 miles, although using the high-flying Mosquito — which could reach over 30,000ft — meant that the Ruhr was covered. Another disadvantage was that the final part of the 'Oboe' run had to be flown straight and level, but, again, the Mosquito's superb performance enabled it to evade the German defences. 'Oboe' was an excellent device, but its limitations meant that it would have to be used by a select group of Pathfinder aircraft rather than as an instrument of the Main Force. **E(MoS) 1439**

Above:
Halifax II BB194/ZA-E of No 10 Squadron undergoes some major engine maintenance at its dispersal at Melbourne, Yorkshire, in December 1942. A close examination of the scene shows fitters working on cylinder blocks on the benches in the foreground, and various engine cowling panels lying on the ground. Such work was routinely carried out in the open, exposed to the vagaries of the British weather. After surviving operations, this aircraft was passed on to No 1658 HCU, but was destroyed in the hands of a 'sprog' pilot in February 1943. **CH 7910**

Right:
A bomb aimer demonstrates the selector switches and bomb release in the cramped nose of another No 10 Squadron aircraft at Melbourne. In early Halifaxes, the bomb aiming was done by the observer or even the wireless operator in some crews. By this date, however, the gradual reorganisation of aircrew tasks in the four-engined types had been completed. The pilot was now assisted by a flight engineer. The navigator — as the observer was now officially known — had been released from his duty of aiming and dropping the bombs. This job was now in the hands of a separate air bomber (or bomb aimer), who also manned the front gun turret when required. The remaining three members of the crew now specialised in their respective tasks, with the gunners no longer receiving wireless training, and the wireless operator no longer having guns to man. These changes contributed to a raised level of professionalism and efficiency within Bomber Command. **CH 7905**

'At long last we were ready and equipped.'

(Sir Arthur Harris, *Bomber Offensive*, 1947)

The war would turn irrevocably against Hitler in 1943, as his forces were pushed back onto the defensive on all fronts. However, the fighting was still remote from Germany's frontiers, and at the beginning of the year Bomber Command remained the only way of striking at the heart of the enemy. Yet, for all the effort thus far expended, the bombing war had made only slow progress. There had been some isolated successes in 1942, but the size and accuracy of the bomber force had been insufficient to cripple German morale decisively. RAF casualties had been severe, and the primary Ruhr targets, blanketed in their ever-present industrial haze, and strongly defended, had escaped significant damage. In 1943 a major growth in the strength and operational effectiveness of Bomber Command would greatly increase the strategic value of the bombing campaign, in which American involvement would become an increasingly important feature. In January, Churchill and Roosevelt, with their Combined Chiefs of Staff, met at Casablanca to discuss future strategy, including the use of their expanding air forces. With the war now firmly in the Allies' favour, a return to the Continent, first through Sicily and Italy, and ultimately via a cross-Channel invasion into France, could now be planned. As far as the strategic bombing offensive was concerned, its primary aim was to be the 'progressive destruction and dislocation of the German military, industrial and economic system, and the undermining of the morale of the German people to a point where their capacity for armed resistance is fatally weakened'. In short, the role of the combined bomber forces of the RAF and the USAAF was to pave the way for the eventual return of Allied armies to Europe.

The so-called 'Casablanca directive', which was sent to Air Chief Marshal Sir Arthur Harris on 4 February, listed various specific target 'systems' for priority attention, including U-boat construction yards, the aircraft industry, communications and oil. However, although the underlying strategic objectives of the directive had been approved by the Combined Chiefs of Staff, Harris and General Ira Eaker, his opposite number commanding the US Eighth Air Force in England, held widely-differing views on its implementation, and both men were given a considerable degree of autonomy in the employment of the forces under their command. The Americans saw merit in attacks on selective targets as specified in the directive, and were keen to extend their daylight precision raids into Germany, but Harris still believed that his general area bombing offensive against industrial cities would be sufficient on its own to bring about the collapse of Germany. At the beginning of 1943, with many improvements in both equipment and tactics in place, he felt confident that

Bomber Command was at last in a position to produce decisive results.

Chief among the new scientific aids available to Bomber Command, 'Oboe' was now in service and promised to bring a hitherto unknown level of accuracy over targets totally obscured by haze or cloud. No 109 Squadron had been chosen to introduce the new equipment for primary target-marking, and in the fast, high-flying Mosquito they had an aircraft perfectly designed for the job. New ground-marking target-indicator bombs, which ejected brightly coloured pyrotechnics just above the ground, would provide a reliable and conspicuous method of visually marking the aiming point. For targets beyond the range of 'Oboe', the bombers had the help of another new device, a ground-scanning radar carried in the aircraft called 'H2S', which had no range limitations and was able to paint a radar image of the ground beneath. Its principal value was as an aid to navigation, assisting in the identification and location of landmarks along the bombers' route, but it could also be used for blind target-marking, although it was far less accurate than 'Oboe' in this regard. Initially, 'H2S' was used by small numbers of Pathfinder aircraft, but would later become a standard fitment in many Main Force squadrons. To make life as difficult as possible for the German defences, two new radio counter-

Below: Lancaster over Hamburg, or 'Chopburg' as the city was more aptly christened by the crews; this famous image of the RAF's bomber offensive was taken on the night of 30/31 January 1943 when 148 aircraft — mostly Lancasters — mounted Bomber Command's 94th raid on the German city. Significantly, it was the first operation which made use of the new radar navigation and blind-bombing aid 'H2S', which was carried in Pathfinder Stirlings and Halifaxes of Nos 7 and 35 Squadrons. On this occasion, however, the attack was not a success, with the bombing being scattered over a wide area. **C 3371**

measures had also just entered operational service. 'Mandrel' was a device — initially ground-based — intended to reduce, by jamming, the range of the German early-warning radar, while 'Tinsel' enabled a bomber's wireless operator to tune into the radio transmissions between enemy fighters and their ground controllers, and drown them out using an engine-mounted microphone.

Two new bomber groups were activated at the beginning of the year. The nine Canadian Wellington and Halifax squadrons, which had formed in the summer and autumn of 1942, became No 6 (Canadian) Group on New Year's Day. A week later, the Pathfinder squadrons were elevated to become No 8 (PFF) Group under Air Vice-Marshal Bennett. As well as these organisational changes, the strength of Bomber Command was also on the verge of a dramatic increase. The conversion programmes which had been set in train during the second half of 1942 had begun to bear fruit, so that in January the majority of Main Force squadrons were fully equipped with four-engined types, giving the force — now numbering over 500 available aircraft — a much greater bomb-hauling capability. The Lancaster was appearing in ever greater numbers, and more effective variants of the Halifax were also reaching the squadrons. By any measure, Bomber Command was an incomparably more formidable weapon than it had been in 1942.

Unfortunately for Harris at this crucial juncture, an upsurge in U-boat activity in the Battle of the Atlantic once again frustrated his plans for Germany. Even before he was sent the

Above: Flying Officer A. Whickham (left), a Mosquito pilot, and his navigator, Pilot Officer W. Makin, pose for an official portrait in the imposing setting of the Air Council Room at the Air Ministry in Whitehall on 31 January 1943, the day after their participation in the first daylight raid on Berlin. Six Mosquitos from Nos 105 and 139 Squadrons bombed the German capital in two attacks, timed to disrupt broadcast speeches by Göbbels and Göring at rallies marking the tenth anniversary of Hitler's accession to power. Damage to the city was insignificant and one aircraft was shot down, but the propaganda value of the raid was immense. **CH 8522**

Casablanca directive, he received orders from the War Cabinet to launch maximum effort raids against the submarine bases on the west coast of France. From January to early March, Bomber Command despatched some 3,000 sorties against Lorient and St Nazaire, but to little effect, since the U-boats were protected by concrete pens, impervious to the bombs used against them. 'We did, in fact, uselessly devastate two perfectly good French towns...' Harris later wrote bitterly. A further diversion of effort resulted from a small number of raids mounted on Italian targets, by order of the Prime Minister who was keen to continue exerting pressure on Hitler's Axis partner to pull out of the war. Turin, La Spezia and Milan were all attacked in February. Despite these diversions, Germany was not ignored. Two operations to Berlin on consecutive nights in the middle of January, using only Lancasters and Halifaxes, were the first raids on the capital for over a year, but the results were disappointing, with the Pathfinders unable to mark the centre of the city and the bombing scattered. Heavy losses were suffered during the second attack when night-fighters caught up with the bomber stream and 22 aircraft were shot down.

Above: Lorient under attack on the night of 4/5 February 1943. Shot from 16,000ft by the light of flares — some of which are visible in the photograph — aircraft can just be made out flying over the target below. Once again the Battle of the Atlantic had diverted attention away from the strategic offensive against Germany; Bomber Command received a directive on 15 January calling for 'maximum effort' attacks on the U-boat bases on the west coast of France. Tragically, the series of area attacks on Lorient and St Nazaire which followed served only to level the French towns, while the U-boats and their personnel remained invulnerable within newly-built concrete 'pens'. **C 3387**

Other German cities, in the Ruhr and beyond, were the targets for important experimental raids using the new pathfinding and marking techniques. On 27/28 January, 'Oboe' Mosquitos used ground-markers for the first time, during a raid on Düsseldorf. The new brightly-burning target-indicators were visible through the thin cloud layer which obscured the target, and which would normally have rendered a successful attack impossible. Two nights later, Stirlings and Halifaxes of the Pathfinder Force carried out the first operational use of 'H2S' over Hamburg, but despite the city's easily discernible radar image, the bombing was disappointingly scattered. Rather more success was achieved at cloud-covered Wilhelmshaven on 11 February when a large naval ammunition depot blew up with dramatic effect. However, the heavy damage inflicted on this occasion would prove to be the exception rather than the rule as far as 'blind' 'H2S' attacks were concerned. The scattered bombing results achieved on the first night of March over Berlin, whose huge expanse saturated the 'H2S' screens with indistinct images, were to prove far more typical. During the first two months after its introduction, 15 major operations using 'H2S' were carried out, but only three caused any appreciable damage to the target. Nevertheless, important lessons were being learned and successful tactics gradually evolving.

In March, Harris was finally able to launch what he described as the 'main offensive', the all-out assault on the industrial cities of Germany. On the night of 5/6 March he sent 442 aircraft on a major raid against Essen, which was to be the opening round in a sustained four-month assault that became known as the 'Battle of the Ruhr'. Thanks to 'Oboe', the weather and industrial haze no longer offered its blanket of protection and the raid was a resounding success, with severe damage caused to the centre of the city and the sprawling Krupps armaments works. It was the first of five major attacks on Essen during the spring of 1943, with other heavy attacks being made on Duisburg, Düsseldorf, Dortmund, Bochum and Wuppertal. In all these raids 'Oboe' was used, mostly with great success, although occasionally scattered bombing occurred when technical problems with the equipment — which were common — prevented the Mosquitos from carrying out their task. The offensive was by no means restricted to the Ruhr towns. In order to prevent the Germans from concentrating their defences, almost half of the attacks during this period were mounted against such widely separated objectives as Berlin, Stettin, Pilsen and Nuremberg; they ranged from single Mosquito nuisance raids to the big Dortmund operation of 23/24 May in which 826 aircraft took part. Attacks beyond the Ruhr, and thus beyond the range of 'Oboe', depended on 'H2S', and consequently bombing results were often disappointing, especially when cloud prevented visual identification of the target.

The Battle of the Ruhr saw Bomber Command operations reach a new level of ferocity, and with it, record losses too. In some 43 major raids carried out over four months, almost 900 bombers were lost. Yet, despite the attrition, Bomber Command emerged at the end of this intensive period of operations with a force considerably greater in numbers than it had at the beginning, an indication of the degree of expansion that occurred during the first half of 1943. Morale, though severely tested during these destructive raids, never sagged; the obvious successes that were being achieved, together with an ample flow of replacements, kept the mood of Harris's force remarkably buoyant. Nevertheless, the heavy casualties prompted attempts to hit back against the Luftwaffe night-fighters. In mid-June, Fighter Command Beaufighters, equipped with radar and a device called 'Serrate', began operations over Europe, using their equipment to home in on the airborne radar of enemy aircraft. However, although contacts were frequent, technical problems and the Beaufighter's lack of range meant that there were relatively few successful interceptions. Later, the Mosquito would take over and excel in this role. Meanwhile, Mosquito fighter-bombers flew the first intruder sorties over enemy fighter bases, seeking to catch the German aircraft when they were at their most vulnerable — during take-off and landing. The Luftwaffe soon learned to fear them, and in time the presence of Mosquitos near their airfields, whether real or imagined, was enough to disrupt severely the activities of the night-fighters.

The Ruhr offensive overshadowed the last operations of No 2 Group before it was transferred to Fighter Command on 1 June, ultimately to become part of the new Second Tactical Air Force.

In their last months of operations with Bomber Command, the Bostons, Venturas and, finally, the Mitchells kept up a programme of intensive daylight attacks against railway targets, power stations and ports in France and the Low Countries. The two Mosquito squadrons, No 105 and No 139, distinguished themselves in daring low-level 'spectaculars' against precision targets and also began night nuisance raids over Germany, operations considered too risky for the vital 'Oboe' Mosquitos. After No 2 Group departed, Bomber Command hung on to both squadrons for the Pathfinders — an indication of the value that Harris placed on the offensive qualities of their superb aircraft and highly trained crews. In contrast, the unloved Lockheed Ventura starred for all the wrong reasons in a memorable action on 3 May, when 11 aircraft of No 487 Squadron, RNZAF, were wiped out in a bungled attack on a power station in Amsterdam. A strong Luftwaffe fighter response overwhelmed the escort and fell on the lumbering bombers, whose leader, Squadron Leader L. Trent, survived long enough to bomb the target before being shot down and captured. He was later awarded the Victoria Cross for his courageous exploit.

Sir Arthur Harris emerged triumphant from the undeniable success of the Battle of the Ruhr, and from his Command's most celebrated operation of the war, No 617 Squadron's masterly 'Dambuster' raid in the middle of May. In contrast, the American daylight offensive was running into serious problems, thanks to increasingly widespread and effective resistance from the German day fighter force. Determined to press on with precision attacks against the target systems identified at Casablanca, the Eighth Air Force had been shocked by the grievous losses it had suffered in its early raids on Germany. As a result, a new directive issued to Harris in early June emphasised that the reduction of the German fighter force was now regarded as essential to the success of the 'Combined Bomber Offensive', or 'Pointblank', as it became known. General Eaker, chief proponent of 'Pointblank', was keen that Bomber Command — not least for its own sake — should join in the offensive against aircraft targets in order to reduce Luftwaffe strength. The Allied chiefs viewed this as fundamental, not only for the success of the air offensive but also as an essential prerequisite for 'Overlord', the proposed invasion of Europe. Harris, however, remained adamant that his force could do little to help in this regard, insisting that he be allowed to continue with his area offensive against German industry and morale. He had no time for the 'panacea-mongers', his term for those who favoured concentrating attacks on a particular type of target, which they claimed would prove decisive. The Combined Bomber Offensive would thus exist only in name, with the Americans attempting to hit selective targets by day and the British continuing with their nightly area attacks on industrial cities. At the end of July and beginning of August, it would be the turn of Germany's second city, Hamburg, to receive the full weight of Bomber Command's destructive power.

In a series of four major raids from 24/25 July to 2/3 August, approximately 3,000 sorties were despatched against Hamburg, devastating the city with a deluge of over 7,000 tons of bombs, of which half were incendiaries. The coastal approach and Hamburg's position on the River Elbe produced clear images on the 'H2S' screens, with the result that the marking and bombing was both accurate and concentrated, especially in the second raid. The damage and loss of life inflicted was by far the worst in the campaign so far. Up to 50,000 people were killed, most in the terrible firestorm which occurred during the second raid, and a million others fled the city. The Germans were genuinely shaken by the fate of Hamburg, with the more realistic in the Nazi hierarchy fearing the worst if Bomber Command's attacks were sustained at this level of intensity. Conversely, Bomber Command enjoyed comparatively light casualties, due to the employment of an anti-radar device called 'Window'. Huge quantities of metallised paper strips were dumped at regular intervals from each aircraft, producing a cloud of false echoes to swamp the enemy radar. At a stroke, the German searchlight, flak and fighter defences were seriously disrupted and only 57 RAF bombers were lost from the three July raids — a casualty rate of only 2.4%. The use of 'Window' had been delayed for 16 months due to fears that the Germans would employ it in attacks against Britain, even though the depleted Luftwaffe bomber arm posed little threat by this stage of the war. It later transpired that the Germans had been well aware of the device long before, refraining from using it for the very same reasons as the British!

Harris was keen to exploit the confusion sown by the surprise use of 'Window' with attacks on other prime targets. On 25 July, the night after the first Hamburg raid, he sent Bomber Command to Essen, which suffered a particularly heavy and concentrated attack. This was followed up on 30 July by a smaller operation to Remscheid, also in the Ruhr. Losses on this occasion, however, were steep as the Germans quickly began to recover from 'Window' and institute new measures to deal with the bombers. The final Hamburg raid at the beginning of August was an even more costly failure, due this time to particularly severe weather which scattered the force and saw a further 29 aircraft fail to return. The German defences were rapidly adapting to the changed conditions. No longer able to direct interceptions by individual aircraft, the ground controllers had turned instead to issuing the night-fighters with a 'running commentary' on the course and height of the bomber stream itself. Once in the stream, it was up to individual German crews to find and attack the bombers on their own. With the development of new airborne radar sets immune to 'Window', these new tactics, called *Zahme Sau* ('Tame Boar'), would prove to be far more effective than the old box system, which had been rendered obsolete by 'Window' and the development of the bomber stream. In provoking a drastic change in the night fighting tactics of the Luftwaffe, Bomber Command had unwittingly sown the seeds of near-disaster in its future operations.

August was Bomber Command's most intensive month of 1943. Mosquitos were despatched on harassing operations to targets in the Ruhr, and there were further Main Force attacks

Right:
Laden with parachutes and flight equipment, a Lancaster crew of No 57 Squadron at Scampton board the van which will take them to dispersal and their waiting aircraft, February 1943. This, and the following three photographs, were part of a sequence taken for another Air Ministry picture story entitled 'T for Tommy Makes a Sortie', which portrayed the events surrounding a single Lancaster bomber and its crew during a typical operation. **CH 8781**

Left:
'T for Tommy's' crew, with their Canadian skipper, Flying Officer J. F. Greenam (in the centre), photographed in front of their aircraft for the night, Lancaster I W4201, which was usually the mount of the squadron CO, Wing Commander F C. Hopcroft (note the Wing Commander's pennant painted below the cockpit). This aircraft had taken part in No 57 Squadron's first Lancaster operation, to Wismar on 12/13 October; it had since completed over 10 more sorties including trips to Le Creusot, Genoa, Turin, Munich, Nuremberg and Berlin. **CH 8648**

Right:
'T for Tommy's' mid-upper gunner, Sergeant 'Dusty' Miller, a 33-year-old former pie salesman, 'scans the sky' for enemy aircraft from the Lancaster's Fraser-Nash FN50 turret. In reality, the shot was taken from the rear emergency ditching hatch on top of the fuselage, while still on the ground at Scampton. The object protruding from the turret below the guns is part of the mechanical taboo track device, which ran along the turret fuselage fairing and prevented the gunner from inadvertently shooting at parts of his own aircraft. **CH 8795**

Below:
The crew of 'T for Tommy' have safely returned from the 'op' and now await interrogation. The bomb aimer, Sergeant 'Bert' Turkentine, a 29-year-old former blacksmith from southeast London (left), and the Canadian navigator, Sergeant 'Muse' Music, aged 21, are offered welcoming cups of tea by an attentive WAAF. **CH 8804**

on cities in northern Italy, once again to hasten Italy's surrender (which occurred in the following month). A notable precision raid was carried out by 596 aircraft on the night of 17/18 August against Germany's secret rocket and flying-bomb research establishment at Peenemünde on the Baltic. The attack was planned in great secrecy (the crews not learning of the true nature of their target until months afterwards) and, in view of the importance and small size of this remote target, was carried out in bright moonlight conditions. In a development of a technique first employed during the Dams raid in May and at Friedrichshafen in June, the raid was directed and controlled on the spot by a 'Master Bomber' aircraft, in this case flown by the CO of No 83 Squadron, Group Captain J. H. Searby, who communicated instructions to the other crews by radio-telephone. Another innovation was the use of 'red spot fire', an improved marker bomb which burned brilliant red and was designed to be easy to recognise, and difficult for the Germans to replicate as a decoy. The raid was a qualified success; considerable damage was caused and a number of key personnel killed, but development of the V-2 rocket was curtailed for only about three months and RAF losses were heavy, a total of 40 bombers failing to return. Some of these were doubtless the result of another innovation, this time on the German side, in the form of upward-firing cannon mounted in some of the night-fighters. This installation, named *Schräge Musik* ('Oblique Music'), enabled the German aircraft to stalk their prey from below, sliding into position in the blind-spot beneath the British bombers before opening fire. The tactic would become devastatingly successful in the months that followed.

Harris had long planned to tackle Berlin as the climax to his main offensive. In late August and early September he tried three major attacks, but these proved costly failures. Target-finding and bombing concentration were hindered by cloudy conditions and problems with 'H2S'; navigators found their screens swamped by a mass of indistinct returns from the sprawling city. Although 'Window' was deployed, 125 aircraft were lost over the course of the three raids, at least 80 of which fell to the guns of the night-fighters — now fully recovered from the disruptions of the early summer. The Stirlings and Halifaxes, with poor operational ceilings of around 13,000ft and 18,000ft respectively,

suffered such heavy casualties in the first two raids that they were stood down for the last operation, which was an all-Lancaster affair. After this mauling, Harris drew back, but his determination to resume the attack in the long nights of the coming winter was undiminished. That autumn he despatched Bomber Command against other 'long-range' targets, with varying results. Hannover escaped major damage on two nights in September, but suffered a crippling attack on a crisp, clear night in early October. Good results were also achieved at Mannheim on 5/6 September, at Frankfurt a month later and Kassel on the night of 22/23 October. This last attack inflicted serious damage on V-1 flying bomb production at the Henschel aircraft works.

In all these attacks, Bomber Command's now standard marking techniques were employed: an initial wave of Pathfinder aircraft with 'H2S' would mark the target area and illuminate it with flares, after which other PFF aircraft would attempt to identify and mark the aiming point visually, using red or green target-indicators (TIs); if the target could not be seen, no markers would be released. Finally, other Pathfinder crews would 'back-up' (re-mark) either the visual markers, if they had been dropped, or if not, the mean point of impact of the TIs released by the blind marker illuminators. The following Main Force crews thus bombed either ground-markers aimed visually (the most accurate form of marking, which was codenamed 'Newhaven') or dropped blind on 'H2S' (less accurate, and known as 'Paramatta'). If all went well, these methods — which only worked in reasonably clear conditions — produced concentrated bombing, but, if the weather intervened, attacks could go astray. When thick cloud over the target prevented the normal target-indicators from being seen, the Pathfinders had to resort to parachute-borne sky-markers, in which case the Main Force were instructed to aim their bombs at the centre of all the flares seen. Owing to the drift of the flares in the wind, normal backing-up could not take place, and 'H2S' aircraft had to remark at intervals throughout the raid. With this, the least accurate technique (codenamed 'Wanganui'), it was difficult to concentrate an attack, and the resultant bombing would often be dispersed and inaccurate.

Bomber Command returned to the German capital on 18/19 November, the opening raid in a concentrated winter assault against the city and other long-distance targets which would be known as the 'Battle of Berlin'. Harris's crews had embarked on their sternest test of the war, an attempt, as the C-in-C put it in a memorable pronouncement, to 'wreck Berlin from end to end'. No-one was in any doubt as to the enormity of the task. The city was a huge, distant target, invariably shrouded in unbroken cloud which made visual identification of the aiming points virtually impossible. The Pathfinders were forced to rely on blind 'H2S' marking — never easy over such a vast urban expanse — and many attacks failed to achieve the necessary degree of bombing concentration. Atrocious weather to and from the target was another obstacle, but the most formidable threat to Bomber Command during those long winter nights was posed by the reorganised German defences. Major diversionary raids or the tactic of sending the bomber stream via an indirect route reduced casualties on some operations, but the 1,150-mile round trips to Berlin involved at least four hours' flying time over enemy territory, and the average loss rate remained stubbornly over 5% — on occasions it was much higher. The Luftwaffe night-fighter force, now reaching the zenith of its powers, was responsible for the vast majority of bomber losses, but other aircraft were taken by the intense flak over the target, or crashed as weary crews attempted to land at fog-shrouded airfields.

At the end of November, the Stirlings of No 3 Group were removed from the offensive, and indeed from all further Main Force bombing operations over Germany. Their pitifully low ceiling had exposed them to the full fury of the enemy defences, and their inability to carry the heavy bombs now routinely used by Bomber Command also put them at a severe disadvantage. The loss *en masse* of these squadrons considerably reduced the strength of Harris's force at a critical time, but by this date in the bombing war the Stirlings were simply obsolete. In the same month, No 100 (Bomber Support) Group was set up to co-ordinate the radio countermeasures effort and to control the operations of intruder and radar-equipped Mosquitos, under-employed in the night defence of the United Kingdom, but now sorely needed in the battle against the Luftwaffe over Germany. Every possible measure was employed to protect the bombers, but as the year ended the balance sheet looked decidedly bleak; in six weeks of operations since the opening of the offensive, a total of 255 aircraft had been lost, from which 1,260 aircrew had been killed. The early optimism had faded and the Battle of Berlin was becoming a slogging match which Bomber Command was losing. In that grim winter, victory seemed a long way off.

Below: A typical area bombing load is displayed within the gaping bomb bay of a No 57 Squadron Lancaster at Scampton, March 1943. A single 4,000lb impact-fused HC 'Cookie' nestles among 12 SBCs, each loaded with 236 4lb incendiary bombs. The various load configurations were given codenames: this, the most commonly deployed for fire-raising, was known as 'Usual'. Incendiary-only loads were referred to as 'Arson'. **CH 18371**

Above:
Wing Commander G. B. Warner (third from left), the CO of No 78 Squadron at Linton-on-Ouse, poses for a publicity shot with his crew, March 1943. Warner's squadron lost 35 bombers between early March and the end of July, during Bomber Command's major offensive against the Ruhr. The aircraft in the background of this photograph, Halifax II W7930/EY-W, was lost while being flown by another crew on 22/23 June during operations to Mülheim.
CH 8902

Above: This Wellington X, HE165 of No 196 Squadron, was damaged by flak during mine-laying operations off the Frisian Islands on the night of 14/15 March 1943, but managed to make a successful emergency landing back at its base at Leconfield, Yorkshire. Airbags have been placed under the wings and a fuel bowser assists in efforts to raise the aircraft onto jacks. The Wellington was successfully repaired and survived for another year, but was written off for good while serving with No 27 OTU at Lichfield, Staffordshire, on 10 April 1944. **CH 10663**

Right:
Lancaster III ED646/PM-V of No 103 Squadron at Elsham Wolds, Lincolnshire, early March 1943. As part of the publicity for 'Wings For Victory Week' (6-13 March), the station photographer was required to supply photographs of the men and machines of the squadron for inclusion in local newspapers. This posed shot, ostensibly depicting the crew setting out on a raid, seems to have been taken in the middle of the day — perhaps before a test flight — judging by the shadows cast by the bright spring sunshine. **CH 8965**

Left:
Inside the aircraft the skipper adopts a suitable pose for the photographer. He is wearing a Type C flying helmet, the most widely used RAF flying helmet of the war and a Type G oxygen mask, which supplied oxygen only when the wearer inhaled, and replaced earlier, wasteful 'constant flow' types. ED646 was flown on some of the key raids of the Battle of the Ruhr between March and July 1943, as well as completing a trip to Hamburg and the famous Peenemünde raid in August. Its luck ran out on the night of 31 August/1 September, when Flying Officer D. Philip and crew were lost without trace after setting out for Berlin. **CH 8971**

Above:
Bombs plunge down onto dockside installations at Brest during 'Ramrod 61' — the attack by 12 Venturas of No 21 Squadron on 3 April 1943. Smoke billows from bomb-bursts which have already straddled the target. A 'Ramrod' was a daylight escorted raid to a specific target in enemy-occupied territory. No 21 Squadron went back to Brest two days later, and struck at shipping in Cherbourg Harbour on 15 April. Altogether it flew a total of 369 sorties with its Venturas between December 1942 and September 1943, losing 10 aircraft in the process. **C 3491**

Right:
'Pinocchio', a veteran Halifax of No 102 Squadron at Pocklington, has the bomb symbol for its 26th operation painted on its fuselage by a member of the ground crew, early April 1943. The ice cream cornets represent raids on Italian targets and the key indicates the aircraft's 21st operation. Surviving this number of trips was no mean feat for a Halifax II, especially in the spring of 1943; No 102 Squadron lost five aircraft in March, five more in April and nine in May. The identity and fate of this particular aircraft is unfortunately unknown. **CH 9331**

Right:
The Battle of the Ruhr was well underway when this photograph was taken of a No 76 Squadron Halifax, W7805/MP-M, being bombed-up at Linton-on-Ouse on 3 April 1943. That night, Bomber Command launched its third raid in a month against Essen, inflicting considerable and widespread damage, at a cost of 21 of the 348 bombers despatched. Twelve Halifaxes, including this one, failed to return and three more crashed over Britain. This aircraft was a Halifax II Series I (Special), an interim design which featured a streamlined Tollerton fairing (named after Tollerton Aircraft Services, which manufactured it) in place of the front turret — one of a number of stop-gap modifications introduced in late 1942 to make the aircraft more aerodynamic. **CH 9158**

Left:
A Mosquito is illuminated by fires and explosions during a dusk attack on the railway workshops at Namur on 6 April 1943. Eight aircraft took part in the attack, one of a number directed against railway installations during this period. No aircraft were lost on this raid, but the Mosquitos were not invulnerable; on previous operations in March a number of aircraft had been intercepted and shot down by Focke-Wulf FW190s. These losses resulted in a decision to broaden Mosquito attack techniques and introduce night operations. No 105 Squadron would fly its first night sorties on 14 April, against Bremen, Hamburg and Wilhelmshaven. **C 3490**

Above: End of an ordeal — the crew of an RAF Air/Sea Rescue launch haul in a dinghy with two exhausted survivors from a No 166 Squadron Wellington, HE862/AS-L, which ditched off the French coast after developing engine trouble on its way to Mannheim on 16 April 1943. Flying Officer R. Lord (facing camera) and Flying Officer E. Hadingham (out of sight) drifted for five days before being picked up. They survived on rainwater, 18 Horlicks tablets and a bar of chocolate between them. The RAF's Air/Sea Rescue organisation, part of Coastal Command after August 1941, faced an ever-increasing workload, but by the end of the war had saved one in three aircrew who ditched or baled out over water. **CH 9389**

Left:
Mosquito IV DZ483/GB-R of No 105 Squadron at Marham about to receive its load of four 500lb bombs, in preparation for a night raid on Berlin, 13 May 1943. In April small numbers of Mosquitos had started making high-level night 'nuisance' and diversionary raids on German cities, including the capital; it was a role for which the aircraft was particularly suited. Although DZ483 returned safely from this operation, it was not so fortunate at the end of the month when it crashed on its return from the Jena raid on 27 May. Flying Officers A. J. Rea and K. S. Bush were both killed. **CH 18009**

Above: While their aircraft are armed, the crews of No 105 Squadron concentrate on the briefing for the night's 'op'. In the foreground are Flying Officer R. G. Hayes DFC (left) and Flight Lieutenant J. Gordon DFC, veterans of many low-level sorties over Germany and occupied Europe, including the first daylight raid on Berlin on 30 January. Sadly, both were to be killed when their Mosquito crashed in Norfolk, attempting to return on one engine from an operation to Leverkusen on 5 November 1943. **CH 18010**

Above: A factory-fresh Halifax II Series IA, HR861, sits in the spring sunshine at the Handley Page plant at Radlett, ready for delivery to the RAF, May 1943. The Series IA, powered by Merlin 22 engines, featured a revised nose, low-profile Boulton Paul dorsal gun turret and other aerodynamic refinements. It was the last in the line of Rolls-Royce-engined Halifaxes and was issued to the squadrons from June 1943. This aircraft was delivered to No 35 Squadron at Graveley, which formed part of No 8 (PFF) Group, but failed to return from an operation to Nuremberg on the night of 10/11 August 1943. **E(MoS)1111**

Left:
A Lancaster of No 617 Squadron releases a 'bouncing bomb' during tests at Reculver in Kent, only days before Operation 'Chastise', the famous raid on the Ruhr dams, which took place on the night of 16/17 May 1943. No 617 Squadron, created specifically for the raid, was equipped with aircraft which had received 'Type 464 Provisioning' modifications (as they were cryptically known by the manufacturer) to accept the special weapon, codenamed 'Upkeep'. The Lancasters had their mid-upper turrets removed, and bomb bays modified to accommodate gear for rotating the weapon to impart backspin, thus assisting its bounce across the water. This photograph was taken from a highly classified (and recently discovered) cine film of the tests, made on either 11 or 13 May. **FLM 2340**

Right:
In another still from the same film, an inert 'Upkeep' 'bomb' crashes ashore onto the beach in front of a group of RAF and civilian officials. Barnes Wallis, inventor of the weapon, is visible on the left of the main group with his arms outstretched. 'Upkeep' was basically a form of depth-charge, weighing 9,250lb and containing 6,600lb of Torpex explosive. It was designed to strike the wall of a dam, sink and then explode against it at a pre-determined depth by means of three hydrostatic pistol fuses. **FLM 2343**

Left:
Après moi, le déluge — water cascades through the breach in the Möhne Dam on the morning after the famous 'bouncing bomb' raid of 16/17 May 1943, carried out by 19 Lancasters of No 617 Squadron, under the command of Wing Commander Guy Gibson. An undoubted technical and propaganda triumph, the operation had less strategic impact than was first thought; the most vital dam, the Sorpe, was not breached nor, probably, could it have been, in view of its method of construction. No 617 Squadron paid a high price; eight aircraft and 56 men failed to return (three survived as POWs). Air Chief Marshal Harris had always been opposed to the raid, but now that it had occurred he refused to disperse the squadron, preferring to keep it in being for future specialist operations. **HU 4594**

Left:
The Dortmund raid of 23/24 May 1943 was Bomber Command's largest non-'Thousand Bomber' raid so far, and the greatest of the Battle of the Ruhr, with 826 aircraft taking part. One of these, a Wellington X of No 431 (Iroquois) Squadron, RCAF, was hit by flak soon after leaving the target area. In the confusion the pilot and rear gunner baled out, but the bomb aimer, Sergeant N. Sloan, took over the controls. With the assistance of the other two crew members still on board, he brought the damaged Wellington back to base, where he landed it safely. Sergeant Sloan, seen here on the left with Flying Officer J. Bailey (WOP/AG) and Sergeant G. Parslow (navigator), was awarded the Conspicuous Gallantry Medal and — unsurprisingly — despatched immediately to pilot training. **CH 10320**

Right:
Wing Commander Guy Gibson VC (right) presents Pilot Officer L. G. Knight, RAAF, to the King during the Royal visit to No 617 Squadron at Scampton on 27 May 1943. During the Dams raid 10 days earlier, Knight's Lancaster had formed part of the first wave of nine aircraft briefed to attack the Möhne Dam. In the event, the dam was breached before he had a chance to bomb, and so he was ordered to fly on to the Eder Dam. His was the third and last mine to be successfully exploded against this target, after which it too was breached. For his part in the operation, Knight was awarded the Distinguished Service Order. On 15/16 September he was killed during another low-level operation by the squadron, this time against the Dortmund-Ems Canal at Ladbergen. **CH 9926**

Right:
The CO of No 139 Squadron, Wing Commander R. W. 'Reggie' Reynolds DSO, DFC (right), with his regular navigator, Flying Officer E. B. 'Ted' Sismore DFC, at Marham in May 1943. On 27 May, Reynolds commanded his squadron on Bomber Command's last spectacular low-level daylight raid, the epic long-distance attack on the optical glass factories at Jena, an operation described at the time as a 'daring attack on the eyes of the *Wehrmacht'*. Six aircraft from No 139 Squadron and eight from No 105 were despatched against a glassworks and the Zeiss optical instrument plant. It was the deepest ever daylight penetration of Germany and, although five aircraft were lost, the target was successfully bombed — a fitting climax to Mosquito operations with No 2 Group. During the raid, Reynolds was wounded in the hand and leg when flak hit his aircraft, and only just managed to bring his damaged Mosquito home.
CH 10135

Right:
The first Lancaster to reach Australia, ED930 'Queenie' was photographed at Prestwick in May 1943, before setting off on its record-breaking 72hr flight via Canada and the USA. After completing a fund-raising tour of Australia, it flew on to New Zealand, setting another record in the process. The aircraft had not flown operationally, and was intended to become the pattern for Lancaster production in Australia, which in the end did not go ahead. Throughout these vast journeys, 'Queenie' was flown by the veteran all-Australian Pathfinder crew seen here, captained by Flight Lieutenant P. Isaacson DFC, DFM (fifth from right). Note the Pathfinder badges worn beneath the aircrew brevets on their breast pockets, and the Coastal Command Fortress in the background. **E(MoS) 1110**

Left:
Happy to be back from 'Happy Valley' — a Halifax crew of No 51 Squadron at Snaith, Yorkshire, hand in their 'chutes to a WAAF in the parachute store after returning from an operation to the Ruhr, probably the raid on Wuppertal on the night of 29/30 May. This operation, carried out by 719 aircraft, was Bomber Command's most successful raid of the Battle of the Ruhr, completely destroying a huge swathe of the town. Almost 3,500 Germans died, by far the heaviest death toll suffered in a single raid to date. **CH 10293**

Above: In June 1943 Leconfield in Yorkshire was home to two No 4 Group squadrons: Nos 196 and 466, RAAF, both equipped with the Wellington X. In this view, 'Y-Young/ers' receives some attention to its engines. The aircraft's name was chosen by its pilot, Pilot Officer R. Young and navigator, Sergeant R. Young! Foaming tankards replace the more usual bomb symbols to indicate 14 successfully completed operations. Note too the squadron number painted on the wheels of the maintenance trestles. **CH 10247**

Left:
'For the want of a nut...' WAAF sparking plug testers at work at Snaith, home to the Halifaxes of No 51 Squadron, June 1943. There were two spark' plugs to each of the twelve cylinders of a Merlin XX engine and therefore 96 plugs to each Halifax (and likewise to each Lancaster). All had to be scrupulously checked and cleaned at regular intervals. The WAAF in the foreground is busy testing the spark, while at the far end of the bench another airwoman notes with an electric pencil on the side of each plug the number of flying hours it has done. After 240 hours' use, plugs were returned to the manufacturer as scrap. **CH 10447**

Above: All aboard for Friedrichshafen. Assisted by two members of the ground crew, Squadron Leader A. M. Hobbs DFC, RNZAF, (second from left) and his crew board their No 9 Squadron Lancaster at Bardney, Lincolnshire, on the evening of 20 June 1943. A force of 56 Lancasters from No 5 Group, led by four Pathfinder aircraft from No 8 (PFF) Group, were detailed to attack the old Zeppelin works at Friedrichshafen on the shore of Lake Constance. This was now the site of the Luftschiffbau radio factory which produced Würzburg radar sets, a crucial part of the German air defence network. As in the recent Dams operation, the attack involved the use of a 'Master Bomber' aircraft to direct the raid, although in the event the bombing was fairly scattered. However, enough aircraft hit the factory to cause considerable damage. To confuse the night-fighters, the force then flew south across the Mediterranean to land at airfields in Algeria. As a result there were no losses that night, but the effort required to stage this first shuttle raid to North Africa meant it was not repeated. A week after this photograph was taken, Squadron Leader Hobbs and crew were all killed when their aircraft was shot down on the way back from Gelsenkirchen. **CH 10403**

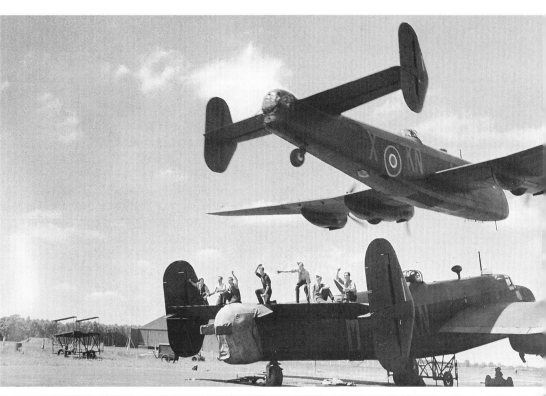

Right:
Low-level 'beat-up' — Halifax II JB911/KN-X of No 77 Squadron roars low over an audience of appreciative 'erks' during air tests at Elvington, Yorkshire, July 1943. A small downwards vision blister, fitted over the ventral well hatch position, can be seen on the underside of the fuselage of both aircraft. Originally devised by personnel of No 76 Squadron, this modification was intended to cover the vulnerable blind spot beneath the bomber which was being increasingly exploited by German night-fighters, and became a standard fitment. Note also the four-gun Boulton Paul mid-upper turrets, then being introduced into service.
CH 10593

Right:
The aircrew and regular ground crew of Lancaster I W4236/QR-K of 'A' Flight, No 61 Squadron, pose with their charge at Syerston on 15 July 1943. 'K-Kitty' had completed 70 operations with barely a scratch — at that point thought to be a Bomber Command record — and was on her third crew, commanded by 23 year-old Pilot Officer W. H. Eager of Winnipeg, Canada (standing, second from left). Although aircrew had come and gone, the same members of the ground staff had kept her in fighting trim since she had been delivered to the squadron on 19 September 1942: seated left to right are LAC W. Long, Corporal C. Bowyer and LAC J. Blackwood. Unfortunately, 'K-Kitty' did not make her century, but finally succumbed to a night-fighter on the night of 9/10 August, when flown by another crew on a trip to Mannheim. **HU 75740**

Above:
Despite the use of 'Window' to confuse airborne and ground radars, 87 British bombers were shot down over enemy territory and another 13 crashed in Britain during the four major raids on Hamburg in July/August 1943. From these, a total of 539 aircrew were killed, including this Polish airman who was found close to the wreckage of his aircraft in Germany on the morning after one of the raids. **HU 13081**

Right:
Another Bomber Command casualty of the assault on Hamburg was this Halifax II of No 78 Squadron, probably JB798/EY-P, which was hit by flak and crashed at Bad Oldesloe, near Lübeck, during the raid of 29/30 July. It was one of two aircraft lost by the squadron that night. Flight Sergeant P. Fraser and crew were all killed. **HU 13165**

Above:
Bomber leaders — the strain of command and operational flying is apparent on the faces of Group Captain Percy Pickard DSO and Bar, DFC (left), Squadron Leader William Blessing DSO, DFC, RAAF, and Group Captain Geoffrey Leonard Cheshire DSO and Bar, DFC, at an investiture at Buckingham Palace, 28 July 1943. Pickard had commanded Wellingtons and Whitleys early in the war, and would be killed leading two Mosquito squadrons on the Amiens Prison raid of 18 February 1944. Blessing received a DSO for his part in the Mosquito raid on the Zeiss optical works at Jena on 27 May 1943. Leonard Cheshire, a former CO of No 76 Squadron, would go on to command No 617 Squadron, complete four operational tours, and be awarded the Victoria Cross for outstanding and sustained courage and leadership. **CH 10706**

Left:
Bomber country — the ancient rhythms of the English landscape continue, undisturbed by the presence of these Halifaxes of an unidentified No 4 Group squadron in Yorkshire, August 1943. Air tests and engine maintenance work take place alongside local farmers gathering in the harvest using a more primitive form of mechanisation.
CH 11098

Above: Halifax crews of No 78 Squadron at Breighton tuck into breakfast after returning from Berlin in the early hours of 1 September 1943. Some are happy to play to the camera, but others seem lost in thought. The raid was the second of three launched by Bomber Command against the 'Big City' between 23/24 August and 3/4 September, but the results were disappointing. Losses, too, were heavy, especially in No 4 Group; No 78 Squadron lost seven aircraft in two operations. **CH 10931**

Above: A Lancaster crew of No 467 Squadron, RAAF, at Bottesford, Leicestershire, prepare to set off for Berlin on the evening of 31 August 1943. They are, from left: Flight Sergeants J. Scott, G. Eriksen and A. Boys, Sergeant C. Adair, Flight Sergeant B. Jones (Captain), Flight Sergeant J. Wilkinson and Sergeant E. Tull, RAF, the only Englishman in the crew. All returned safely, but Sergeant Adair was killed less than a month later, flying as rear gunner in another aircraft. Their veteran aircraft, ED547/PO-M, survived almost a year of operations with the squadron before succumbing to the German defences on the night of 29/30 December, during another operation to Berlin. **AUS 1760**

Above: The crew of the first Canadian-built Lancaster X to arrive in Britain, KB700, christened the 'Ruhr Express', photographed with their mascot on arrival at Northolt, Middlesex, on 15 September 1943. They are, left to right: Squadron Leader Reg Lane DSO, DFC (pilot), Pilot Officer Johnny Carrere (navigator), Sergeant Ross Webb (WOP/AG), Flight Sergeant Reg Burgar (mid-upper gunner) with 'Bambi', Pilot Officer Steve Boczar (second pilot), Flight Sergeant R. Wright DFM (bomb aimer), and Sergeant Mike Baczinski (flight engineer). The 'Ruhr Express' was initially delivered to No 405 (Vancouver) Squadron, RCAF, but soon went on to No 419 (Moose) Squadron, RCAF, at Middleton St George, where it was eventually destroyed in a landing accident returning from Nuremberg, its 49th operational sortie, on 3 January 1945. **CH 11042**

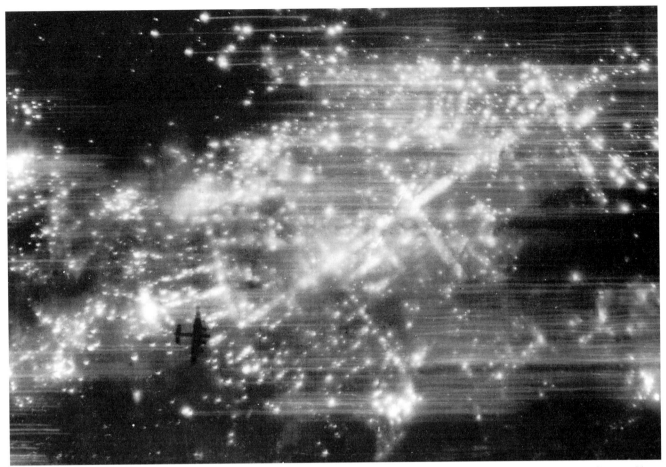

Above: A Lancaster is silhouetted over the fires of Hannover on the night of 8/9 October 1943, during the most devastating raid of the war on the city. Clear conditions helped the Pathfinders to mark the target accurately, and the bombing that followed was very concentrated. The attack was also the last Bomber Command bombing operation in which the veteran Wellingtons took part, with 26 aircraft being despatched by No 300 (Masovian) and No 432 (Leaside) Squadrons. **C3898**

Above: The wreckage of a Halifax, shot down in the early hours of 9 October 1943, during the raid on Hannover. The fine weather which aided the Pathfinders' marking also assisted the German night-fighter force, which had a successful night, claiming many of the 29 Lancasters and Halifaxes which did not make it back from the operation. Two more bombers crashed on their return. **HU 25829**

Left:
This bizarre scene was the result of a night flying accident at No 19 OTU, Kinloss, Morayshire, on 19 October 1943, when an Avro Anson, DJ104/XK-K, managed to land on top of Whitley V N1369/UO-U, which was waiting to take off. No injuries were reported but the Whitley was written off. No 19 OTU was formed in May 1940 for night bomber crew training, and took part in the 'Thousand Bomber' raids to Cologne and Bremen in 1942 (during which the Whitleys operated from Abingdon). Due to the high ground and frequent bad weather at this northerly Scottish location, the unit suffered a higher than average accident rate, losing approximately 200 aircrew during the war. **HU 54488**

Right:
A sergeant on flying control duty reports in as a Halifax V of No 1663 HCU comes in to land, 21 October 1943. Note the propeller spinners, which appear to be painted red and white. The location is Holme-on-Spalding Moor, Yorkshire, although No 1663 HCU was actually based at Rufforth, four miles west of York, from March 1943 until the end of the war. At this date there were 19 heavy conversion units in existence, distributed among the various bomber groups. **CH 11528**

Above:
No 76 Squadron Halifax crews at Holme-on-Spalding Moor gather near the transport which will take them out to their aircraft for the Kassel raid of 22/23 October 1943. This was one of the most devastating attacks on a German city since the Hamburg firestorm raid in July. A huge area of the city was destroyed, and all three Henschel aircraft factories which were making V-1 flying bombs were severely damaged, disrupting production of Hitler's 'vengeance weapons'. Bomber Command suffered heavily too; 44 out of 569 aircraft failed to return, including one from No 76 Squadron. **CH 11401**

Above: 'Corona' operators of No 80 Wing at West Kingsdown, Kent. 'Corona' was a radio jamming and deception countermeasure intended to disrupt German high-frequency ground-to-air communications, in particular the 'running commentary' which gave night-fighter crews instructions as to the whereabouts of the bomber stream. It was first used when Bomber Command went to Kassel on 22/23 October 1943, and supplemented simple airborne noise jammers such as 'Tinsel', which used microphones placed in aircraft engine nacelles. Using four high-power transmitters, 'Corona' broadcast spurious instructions to the German night-fighter crews, employing German-speaking WAAFs to imitate female ground controllers when the Germans tried that ruse. The gramophone turntable visible in the photograph was for 'jumbled-voice' jamming. Such measures, although never able to 'blind' Germany's air defence control system totally, certainly helped reduce its effectiveness. **CH 16682**

Left:
A Halifax II Series IA, HR952/MH-X of No 51 Squadron, is refuelled and bombed-up with incendiaries and 500-pounders at Snaith, in a photograph officially released in November 1943, but which may have been taken earlier in the year. The long, streamlined forward fuselage introduced with this variant helped to increase the aircraft's performance, but the single Vickers gas-operated machine gun fitted in the nose transparency was of questionable value. Later transferred to No 10 Squadron, this Halifax was lost on the night of 28/29 January 1944 during a typically costly raid on Berlin. **CH 11622**

Right:
A sombre Stirling crew during interrogation at Mildenhall, following their return from the Berlin raid of 22/23 November 1943. Seated left to right are: Pilot Officer R. Brown (pilot), Sergeant W. Brodie (flight engineer), Sergeant F. Forde (wireless operator), Flight Sergeant P. Harwood (bomb aimer) and Sergeant F. Tidmas (navigator). This was the last bombing operation over Germany in which Stirlings participated. With Bomber Command's all-out assault on the German capital less than a week old, the C-in-C decided that the Stirlings of No 3 Group would have to be withdrawn. Their inability to match the altitudes flown by the Lancasters and Halifaxes exposed them to the full weight of flak and fighters, and over recent months losses had become intolerable. **CH 11640**

Right:
Safely back at Skellingthorpe, Lincolnshire, this No 50 Squadron crew, commanded by Flying Officer J. Lees, RCAF (standing left), were photographed in front of their battle-scarred Lancaster, 'O-Orange', after returning from Leipzig on 4 December 1943. The Lancaster had been raked by fire from a night-fighter, which knocked out the flaps, damaged both gun turrets and shot part of the tailplane away. Undaunted, Lees and his crew bombed the target and then brought their aircraft home to base. Note the holes in the fuselage, made by the night-fighter's 20mm cannon shells. **CAN 4032**

Right:
Another bomber which only just made it back after tangling with a night-fighter was Halifax II HR868/MH-B of No 51 Squadron, which was attacked on its way to Frankfurt on the night of 20/21 December 1943. The bomb aimer was killed, and a fire started in the bomb bay, which fortunately blew itself out. Unable to jettison the bombs, the crew were forced to bring them back to Snaith. Despite the extensive damage, HR868 was repaired and flew again, eventually going on to serve with No 1656 HCU. It was one of the few Halifaxes delivered during this period that survived the war. Note the aerial for the 'Monica' tail warning radar below the rear turret. Introduced in early 1943, this device was designed to detect night-fighters approaching from behind, but the Germans were quick to design equipment for their fighters which actually homed in on it — a horrifying fact that was not discovered until the middle of 1944. **CE 113**

The basic tactics of Bomber Command which had been pursued with vigour and increasing effectiveness since March 1942 were now, at last, in March 1944, severely checked by the hitherto unparalleled ascendancy of the German night-fighter force.'

(Official History, HMSO, 1961)

1944 was invasion year for the Allies, the culmination of months of planning and preparation which would see British, Canadian and American forces embark on the greatest amphibious operation in history, the assault on Hitler's 'Fortress Europe'. So important was the success of this great enterprise that, during the spring and summer, operational control of Bomber Command (and the US strategic air forces in Europe) would be placed under the overall command of the Supreme Allied Commander, General Dwight D. Eisenhower. Tactical support for the Normandy invasion and the Allied lodgement in France would be Bomber Command's ultimate diversion, and would usher in the beginnings of a dramatic turnaround in the fortunes of the bomber crews, who in the spring of 1944 were emerging from the nightmare of the Battle of Berlin. As the year progressed, Bomber Command would reach a level of operational efficiency and destructive power unimaginable only a couple of years before. Its front-line strength would increase dramatically with the formation of many new squadrons, and — of most concern to the crews — in the autumn there would be a sharp decline in the loss rate as the German defences were overwhelmed. Perhaps the most staggering statistic is that, at the beginning of the year, 85% of the total bomb tonnage dropped by Bomber Command had yet to be delivered! The famous 'battles' of 1943 — the Ruhr, Hamburg, even Berlin — were but an overture to the main act of the bombing offensive, which had yet to be played out.

In January 1944, however, there were few hints of the better times ahead, and the scales appeared decisively tipped in favour of the German night-fighter force. Midway through Air Chief Marshal Harris's sustained winter assault on the enemy capital, Bomber Command losses were reaching crisis point. The average missing rate for the month, which saw nine major operations including six to Berlin, was just over 6%. On some operations the casualty figures were much higher — at Brunswick on the night of 14/15 January the loss rate was 7.6%, and at Magdeburg, a week later, it reached 8.8%. Particularly badly affected were the No 4 Group squadrons operating the inferior Mk II and V Halifaxes which, with the Stirlings taken off operations, were now the most vulnerable aircraft in the force, and suffering appallingly as a result; Pocklington-based No 102 Squadron was especially hard hit towards the end of the

month, when five crews failed to return from Berlin on 20/21 January, and four more were lost going to Magdeburg the following night. The Lancaster crews, who were by now bearing the brunt of the offensive, were only marginally better off. Altogether, 353 aircraft on bombing or mine-laying sorties failed to return, or were written off in crashes, during this terrible month — Bomber Command's worst of the war — and over 2,000 aircrew were killed.

The planners tried their best to minimise the losses; diversionary attacks and feint routing of the Main Force had become standard tactical methods, but the German controllers were rarely deceived for long. In an effort to give the Luftwaffe as little time as possible to react, the duration of attacks was reduced, but increased concentration over the target also increased the chance of losses due to collisions and hits by falling bombs. 'Window' was dropped in huge quantities, but its value was now greatly reduced by the introduction of new German airborne radar sets immune to its effects. Various radio counter-measures continued to be deployed, but no amount of jamming or issuing of spurious instructions to enemy pilots over the airwaves could prevent the Germans from feeding their night-fighters into the bomber streams, often long before targets were reached. Once their quarries had been located, the contest was seldom in doubt, as a graphic passage in the Official History testifies: 'Belching flame from their exhausts as well as radar transmissions from their navigational and fighter warning apparatus made [the bombers] all too apparent to those who hunted them. Once engaged in combat, they had little chance of victory and not much of escape, while the large quantities of petrol, incendiary bombs, high explosives and oxygen with which they were filled often gave spectacular evidence of their destruction. Outpaced, outmanoeuvred and outgunned by the German night-fighters and in a generally highly inflammable and explosive condition, these black monsters presented an ideal target...'

By February, the assault on Berlin was petering out. It was becoming increasingly clear that Bomber Command's attacks on the capital were having little or no impact in weakening Germany's resolve to continue the war, despite the considerable amount of damage that was being inflicted. Harris's force had been dashing itself against a target which was simply too big, too far away and too well defended to be subjugated in the way of Essen or Hamburg in 1943. The penultimate Berlin operation was carried out on 15/16 February when 891 aircraft — the largest force so far despatched to the city — dropped a record 2,642 tons of bombs, causing further widespread damage. A greater proportion of Bomber Command's effort was now being directed towards cities in southern Germany, including important 'Pointblank' targets such as Stuttgart, Leipzig and Frankfurt. The defences were no less ferocious. A major raid on

Above: Lancaster I R5729/KM-A of No 44 Squadron at Dunholme Lodge, Lincolnshire, before setting out for Berlin on 2 January 1944. This aircraft was a veteran of more than 70 raids over enemy territory, the first being to Duisburg in July 1942. It eventually failed to return from Brunswick on 14/15 January, barely two weeks after this photograph was taken, with the loss of Flight Sergeant K. Curatolo, RCAF, and all his crew. Note the F24 bombing camera protruding from the bomb aimer's compartment just in front of the bomb bay. **CH 11929**

Above: Back from Berlin — weary crews of No 44 Squadron gather for interrogation at Dunholme Lodge in the early hours of the morning, 3 January 1944. The Battle of Berlin was at its height, but this raid was largely ineffective, and little damage was caused for the loss of 27 aircraft from a force of 383 despatched. Everyone from No 44 made it back on this occasion, but the squadron was to finish the war with the heaviest Lancaster losses in the whole of Bomber Command. **CH 11924**

Leipzig on 19/20 February was particularly harrowing for the bomber crews when the night-fighters infiltrated the stream at an early stage in the outward flight. To make matters worse, mistakes made in calculating wind strengths meant many bombers arrived at Leipzig before the Pathfinders and were forced to orbit the target, whereupon 20 were shot down by flak and a further four lost in collisions. Altogether, 82 aircraft failed to return or were damaged beyond repair — 9.5% of the force. The long-suffering Halifaxes endured a typically grim night, losing almost 15% of their number, as a result of which Harris finally decided to withdraw all but the superior Hercules-powered Halifax IIIs from operations to Germany.

In the aftermath of this disaster, Bomber Command struck at two more key targets identified in the 'Pointblank' directive. On 24/25 February Harris relented to American pressure and sent his crews to Schweinfurt, home of Germany's vital ball-bearing industry, following up the next night with an attack on Augsburg, location of the MAN engineering works and other important factories connected with the German aircraft industry. This latter attack was almost too accurate, with most of the bombing concentrated in the less industrial, but more densely-packed, mediæval centre of the city, with predictably destructive results. As February gave way to March, the US Eighth Air Force finally joined in the offensive against Berlin, its aircraft appearing over the city in strength on 6 March. Harris had called for American help months before, but, after crippling deep-penetration raids in the summer and autumn of 1943, the USAAF had chosen to await the arrival of their outstanding P-51 Mustang escort fighters before contemplating such an assault. The cruel irony of the situation now was that, thanks to the presence of escort fighters, USAAF losses incurred when raiding Berlin in daylight, even on their worst days, were less than those suffered at night by Bomber Command.

On 24/25 March, Harris despatched his final Main Force operation of the war against the German capital, but once again the bombing was scattered and losses heavy. Strong winds fragmented the force of 811 bombers and 74 of them failed to return, many this time falling to flak as they wandered hopelessly off-track over heavily defended areas such as the Ruhr. Barely a week later, on the last night of the month, 94 bombers were shot down and 11 more destroyed in crashes during an ill-fated operation to Nuremberg, an infamous raid that combined bad luck with uncharacteristically bad operational planning to produce Bomber Command's worst night of the war. Almost 12% of the force that set out was destroyed and 537 aircrew were killed (more than the total number of pilots who died in the Battle of Britain). On 7 April, in a statement that came as close as he was prepared to go towards admitting defeat, Sir Arthur Harris informed the Air Ministry 'that the strength of German defences would in time reach a point at which night bombing attacks by existing methods and types of heavy bomber would involve percentage casualty rates which could not in the long run be sustained'. Many would argue that that time had already come.

In early December 1943, Harris had predicted that, providing he received sufficient numbers of Lancasters, he could '...produce in Germany by April 1st 1944, a state of devastation in which surrender is inevitable'. Unfortunately, no such event had occurred. Instead, after a gargantuan effort, Bomber Command found itself reeling from its most serious defeat of the war. The effects of geography, the weather, and, above all, the German defences had conspired to blunt the assault. Since November 1943, Bomber Command had taken part in 32 major area attacks, including 16 against Berlin, losing over 1,000 aircraft — more than the equivalent of its entire available strength. Great swathes of the city had been reduced to rubble, but Berlin had weathered the storm unleashed against it (though it would continue to be tormented by a less intensive bombardment from the Mosquitos of the Light Night Striking Force until the end of the war). Just as the German day fighters had virtually halted long-range attacks by the US Eighth Air Force in the previous autumn, the German night-fighters had now made deep penetrations of Reich airspace even more costly for Bomber Command. Yet, despite the attrition, Harris never wanted for replacement crews or aircraft, and the most crippling losses could be made good almost immediately. It was the drain of experienced crews, though, that had become unsustainable and which posed the most serious threat to the effectiveness of his force. To the great credit of the crews, morale on the squadrons had held up well throughout this hellish period, due in no small measure to Harris's own brand of leadership, but, after the failure of the Berlin offensive, and the disasters of Magdeburg, Leipzig, and Nuremberg, the tactical doctrine of sending the whole force on repeated attacks against single, distant targets was in tatters.

Fortunately for Harris's weary crews, Bomber Command operations were about to take a new direction as Allied attention focused on Operation 'Overlord', the forthcoming invasion of Normandy. The role of the air forces in this endeavour had long been a subject of contention; no-one disputed the requirement for air superiority over the invasion area, but the need to prevent the enemy from concentrating his forces against the beachhead was more problematic. Air Chief Marshal Sir Trafford Leigh-Mallory, who commanded the fighters and light bombers of the Allied Expeditionary Air Force, had advocated a plan to paralyse the French rail network before the invasion took place. Since his own force, which lacked a heavy bomber component, was insufficient for this purpose he looked to Bomber Command and the US Eighth Air Force to supply the necessary bomb-lifting effort. But neither Harris nor General Carl Spaatz, commanding the US strategic air forces in England and Italy, was keen to divert his forces from the strategic assault on Germany, while others — including Churchill — were haunted by the prospect of the numerous civilian casualties which might result from heavy attacks on French targets. As something of an experiment, therefore, Harris had been ordered in early March to begin a series of attacks on various key marshalling yards, the destruction of which would immobilize enemy railway traffic in the area immediately behind the coast. As these targets were located in populous areas, accuracy was vital, and attacks were to

be carried out using ground-marking techniques in moonlit periods only. In the event, operations against Paris-Trappes, Le Mans, Amiens, Laon and Aulnoye, carried out mostly by the older Halifaxes and Stirlings, proved more successful than anyone had imagined, and convinced the Allied commanders that the 'Railway Plan' would work.

Harris nevertheless deplored any diversion from the continuation of his area bombing campaign, while Spaatz pressed for attacks on Germany's synthetic oil plants, which he considered — rightly, as it turned out — to be the enemy's Achilles' heel. But 'Overlord' was far too important to be compromised by individual differences of opinion, and on 14 April Bomber Command and the US strategic air forces were officially placed under the control of the Supreme Headquarters Allied Expeditionary Forces (SHAEF), to afford direct support for the invasion of Europe. The reduction of enemy air combat strength — largely in the hands of the American daylight offensive — and the disruption of enemy rail communications into the 'Overlord' lodgement area were now the prime objectives of the bomber fleets. Operations against the French railway system would thus continue, with the burden of the assault falling to Bomber Command. 'The panacea merchants had triumphed,' Harris wrote later; 'Naturally I did not quarrel with the decision to put the bomber force at the disposal of the invading army once the die had been cast; I knew that the armies could not succeed without them.'

Despite earlier worries, the majority of attacks on railway targets in France were carried out with outstanding accuracy. In the opening attacks of March and early April, over half the

Above: Safely back on the ground at Bardney, there is time for a smoke for a member of this No 9 Squadron crew just back from Stettin, 6 January 1944. A successful Mosquito diversionary attack on Berlin kept the casualties down to a moderate — by the standards of the time — 4.5%. W4964/WS-J was another long-lasting Lancaster, beginning operations in April 1943 and going on to complete a total of 106 sorties, before being pensioned off as a ground instructional airframe in December 1944. **CH 11972**

bombers were achieving hits within 700yd of the aiming point when bombing from medium altitudes on markers placed by 'Oboe' Mosquitos. No 5 Group, operating as an independent force, went one better and became particularly adept at precision attacks using an even more accurate low-level marking technique pioneered earlier in the year by the CO of No 617 Squadron, Leonard Cheshire. On 8/9 February he had demonstrated his ideas by dropping incendiaries at rooftop height onto the Gnome-Rhône aero-engine factory at Limoges, prior to a devastating attack by 11 other Lancasters from 10,000ft using huge 12,000lb bombs. On 5 April, this time flying a Mosquito, Cheshire repeated his success by carrying out a similarly dramatic marking of an aircraft factory in Toulouse; diving at the target, he aimed his markers accurately using the aircraft's gunsight. These were quickly backed-up by two of his squadron's Lancasters, before another 142 aircraft arrived to flatten the factory, with minimal French casualties.

No 5 Group continued to refine its technique, producing startling results in attacks on the marshalling yards at Juvisy in Paris on 18/19 April, and, two nights later, at La Chapelle, north of the French capital. The new methods reduced the average bombing error to less than 300yd, and were applied equally effectively to more heavily defended targets, as proved by

Cheshire again on 24/25 April, when he successfully marked the centre of Munich despite intense flak and searchlights. On occasions, however, attempts to ensure extreme accuracy cost the bombers dear. Things went seriously wrong on the night of 3/4 May, when 346 Lancasters were sent to a German military depot at Mailly-le-Camp. The low-level marking was very accurate, but radio problems plaguing the Master Bomber's Mosquito meant that the order to bomb could not be transmitted to the rest of the force orbiting the target. The ensuing delay was long enough for the German night-fighters to arrive on the scene, with terrible consequences; 43 Lancasters were shot down.

Bomber Command's attacks on railway targets were undoubtedly of great importance; they produced a growing paralysis of movement in northern France which hindered German reactions to the invasion when it came. Interspersed with these operations, raids continued against German cities, many with aviation-related industries, but in May almost 80% of the Command's effort was directed against invasion targets in France and Belgium. In the last few weeks before D-Day, operations were extended to include strikes on ammunition dumps, army camps and airfields. To disguise the Allies' intentions in Normandy, and to maintain the deception that the invasion would be in the Pas de Calais, an equal or greater weight of ordnance had to be dropped on targets at locations further north along the coast. For the final 'softening-up' in the days just before the landings, Bomber Command was joined by the American 'heavies' and the fighter-bombers of the Allied tactical air forces in attacks on coastal gun batteries and radio and radar stations.

On 5/6 June, the eve of D-Day, Bomber Command flew 1,211 sorties, the highest total for a single night of the war so far. A record 5,000 tons of bombs were deposited, almost all on coastal artillery batteries and defensive positions. For some crews, returning in the early morning light, there was the spectacle of the greatest naval armada in history slowly approaching the Normandy coast. Meanwhile, 60 miles to the east, in a part of the Allied deception plan called Operation 'Taxable', aircraft of No 218 and No 617 Squadrons flew a carefully rehearsed pattern of drifting orbits over the Channel, dispensing clouds of 'Window' and gradually moving towards the French coast to simulate the approach of a large fleet moving at eight knots. The real invasion force was screened by aircraft of No 199 Squadron, flying 'Mandrel' jamming sorties against the German long-range 'Freya' radars. Twenty-four hours later, the Allies were ashore in Normandy. In the following weeks, Bomber Command delivered a huge quantity of high-explosives to various tactical targets in France, including lines of communications, supply depots and troop positions. Meanwhile, strikes on railway targets behind the immediate

Below: Pilot Officer V. A. Reed DFM, a gunnery instructor with one tour of 'ops' behind him, points out the essential recognition characteristics of the Short Stirling to an assembly of air gunners on a refresher course at an unidentified gunnery school, January 1944. It will never be known how many British bombers were fired upon in error by tired or nervous gunners in other aircraft, but it did occur, and casualties were inflicted. **CH 12153**

battlefront continued, and from mid-June a major diversionary campaign against V-weapon storage and launching sites in northern France got underway, to counter the alarming but inconsequential threat of Hitler's flying-bombs. For Bomber Command, it was proving to be a summer of unparalleled intensity and variety.

Until now, Bomber Command had remained firmly wedded to night attacks, but the operational situation was changing rapidly, and on 14 June Harris authorised the first major Main Force daylight raid since October 1942. For this experimental operation, E-boats and other German light naval forces sheltering in Le Havre were bombed during an evening attack. Despite the C-in-C's worries about Luftwaffe opposition, the force was well protected by RAF fighters and only one Lancaster was lost — to flak. Henceforth, daylight attacks against French targets would become increasingly frequent, the umbrella of overwhelming Allied air superiority easily able to protect the bombers against the feeble and sporadic resistance put up by the decimated German day fighter force. In contrast, night operations could still prove costly, with the German night-fighters in France reinforced and able to operate virtually unopposed. In a night of intensive operations against various V-weapon sites on 24/25 June, 22 Lancasters fell to their guns. On 7/8 July, 32 Lancasters were lost from 221 aircraft attacking a flying-bomb storage site. Two squadrons, No 106 and No 207, lost five crews apiece on that night.

June saw the first of a series of Bomber Command raids on German synthetic oil plants in the Ruhr, another 'panacea' target to which Harris was opposed, but which General Spaatz, and

many in the Air Ministry including the Chief of the Air Staff, Sir Charles Portal, were convinced represented the key to crippling the German war machine. The Americans had made a start on their oil offensive in May, able at last to fly deep-penetration missions with Mustang escorts which inflicted a heavy toll on the Luftwaffe fighters that came up to challenge them. In support, and when his priorities over France allowed, Harris was invited to contribute a portion of his effort against 10 oil plants in the Ruhr. Once again, though, the very different tactical situation at night meant that Bomber Command's initial attacks were costly affairs. The raid on the Nordstern plant at Gelsenkirchen on 12/13 June was extremely accurate and inflicted massive damage, but saw 17 Lancasters — just over 6% of the force — shot down. Two further raids that month, on Sterkrade/Holten and Wesseling, also resulted in terrible losses. In the latter attack, 38 Lancasters were lost.

One major advantage brought by the RAF's involvement in the oil campaign was that the Lancasters' prodigious loads, and their bigger bombs, inflicted greater and more permanent destruction to plant machinery than the lesser quantities of relatively lightweight ordnance dropped by the Americans. Furthermore, advances in night bombing techniques and

Below: Graphic evidence of a one-sided struggle is provided by Lancaster DV305 'O-Oboe' of No 550 Squadron, which Flying Officer G. Morrison brought in to the emergency landing ground at Woodbridge in Suffolk, after being attacked by a night-fighter over Berlin on the night of 30/31 January 1944. Both gunners were mortally wounded by a hail of machine gun and cannon fire from the enemy aircraft, and one member of the crew baled out in the confusion. The badly-damaged Lancaster was declared a write-off. **CE 121**

improved versions of its blind-bombing aids meant that Bomber Command could now hit targets as small as individual oil plants with an impressive degree of accuracy. 'Precision bombing on markers dropped by 'Oboe' in average weather proved far more effective than we had any right to expect,' Harris wrote later. Losses to night-fighters remained the main problem, despite the best efforts of No 100 Group's Mosquitos and other counter-measures, and this prompted the extension of daylight attacks into Germany itself. On 27 August, 243 heavily escorted bombers — mostly Halifaxes — attacked the oil refinery at Homberg/Meerbeck. It was the first major Bomber Command daylight operation on a German target since the Blenheim raid on the Cologne power stations in August 1941. Despite intense flak, there were no losses, and the Spitfire escorts drove away the single enemy fighter which offered resistance. Bomber Command had finally achieved its long-held ambition of raiding the Ruhr in daylight hours.

In addition to his oil and tactical objectives, Harris secured permission from SHAEF to mount occasional city attacks with his surplus forces, and in the late summer his bombers fell on targets such as Kiel, Stettin, Frankfurt, Stuttgart and Königsberg. The attack on the last of these, on 29/30 August, when a mere 189 Lancasters of No 5 Group demolished some 40% of the city's housing and 20% of its industry, graphically demonstrated the vastly improved power and accuracy of Bomber Command; only a small number of aircraft was now required to create awesome levels of destruction. A similarly effective raid was carried out a fortnight later against Darmstadt, a virgin target which was virtually destroyed by 226 Lancasters, for the loss of 12 aircraft. Meanwhile, the debate over the most effective use of the heavy bomber force was further complicated by the Deputy Supreme Commander, Air Chief Marshal Sir Arthur Tedder, who argued for an extension of the railway campaign to Germany. Keen to find a target system against which both the strategic and tactical air forces could contribute attacks — a 'common denominator' system — Tedder saw railway and canal communications as Germany's weak link. Concentrating on her transport infrastructure would, he suggested, both impede the movement of her armies, thus assisting the Allied advance, and contribute decisively to the dislocation of her industrial activity, which was an underlying aim of the strategic bombing offensive.

However, despite the merits of the so-called 'Transport Plan', and Harris's own forthright views, it was the oil campaign, favoured by both Portal and Spaatz, and now known to be having dramatic effects on German fuel production, that won the day. On 25 September, Bomber Command and the American strategic air forces received a directive to concentrate their attacks on the German petroleum industry, with rail and canal communications, and tank and vehicle production as joint second priorities. Bomber Command had now been officially released from SHAEF control, but would remain on hand to support the ground forces in future operations. However, optimism that the war might end before Christmas had evaporated by the end of September following the failure of Operation 'Market Garden' at Arnhem, and the stalling of the Allied advance on the frontiers of Germany in the face of strengthening resistance. This slow-down in the land offensive prompted further argument about the role of Bomber Command. For Harris, the situation was clear enough. Over and above any other tactical or strategic objectives assigned to his still-expanding force, it was, he maintained, only the continued assault on the enemy's industrial cities that offered the surest way to precipitate the long-awaited German collapse. He would continue to pursue this course whenever he could.

The bomber offensive was about to reach a climax. In the final quarter of 1944, Bomber Command dropped over 150,000 tons of bombs on German targets, more than the amount dropped in the whole of 1943! At least half of this total was aimed at industrial cities. In early October, Harris began a second offensive against the Ruhr, but this time the odds were stacked in favour of the RAF bombers rather than the defences. The German night-fighter force, deprived of its forward bases and radar sites by the Allied advance, and subjected to fuel shortages and constant attrition by Allied fighters strafing its airfields, was beginning to crumble. As a result, Bomber Command's night losses fell dramatically. In the opening attack, on Dortmund on 6/7 October, only five aircraft failed to return from a force of 523, despite perfect moonlit conditions. The destruction wrought by these raids on familiar industrial centres, which had been visited by Bomber Command so often before, was now on an unsurpassed scale.

In the middle of October, in an operation designed to impress on the enemy the awesome power of the Allied Air Forces, over 2,000 bomber sorties were despatched against Duisburg in less than 48 hours, saturating the city with almost 9,000 tons of bombs. On 23/24 October, Essen received its heaviest attack of the war so far when over 4,500 tons of bombs rained down. Production at the Krupps complex all but ceased after this raid. As in other attacks on such targets, the vast majority of the bombs now used were high-explosives rather than incendiaries; by this stage there was little left to burn, and the heavier bombs ensured that the destruction was unrepairable. Whatever the morale effects of the Ruhr attacks in these last three months, the material devastation caused by some 60,000 tons of bombs was undoubtedly contributing to the slow death of German industry. On 11 November, Hitler's Armaments Minister, Albert Speer, informed his increasingly remote leader that the situation there had reached crisis point, with many prime heavy industries breaking down, either through direct damage or lack of supplies.

In accordance with the September directive's primary objective, Harris continued attacks on oil targets when weather and the tactical situation allowed. They were stepped up in November as a result of a new directive, and some prompting from Portal, who was keen for Bomber Command to play a greater part in the campaign which seemed to be having the most decisive effect. Important operations were also despatched against railway targets, enemy garrisons holding out in the

Channel ports and German towns in the path of the Allied advance. The skills of the precision specialists of No 5 Group were graphically demonstrated by finally despatching the *Tirpitz*, and repeatedly breaching those vital conduits of German industrial traffic, the Dortmund-Ems and Mittelland Canals. Above all, however, Bomber Command maintained its punishing attacks on German industry and morale. Cities such as Brunswick, Wilhelmshaven and Bremen suffered their final and most damaging raids as the area offensive attained new levels of destructiveness.

Even a blanket overcast now failed to protect Germany's beleaguered cities, thanks to a new addition to Bomber Command's technological armoury. No 3 Group had been chosen to equip with a new blind-bombing device called 'G-H', which operated on the same principle as 'Oboe', except that the initial radio pulse transmissions were made by the aircraft rather than the ground stations; this enabled many more aircraft to use it simultaneously. As with 'Oboe', mobile 'G-H' transmitters had followed the advancing Allied ground forces into Europe, thereby increasing the area of coverage over Germany. By October, a quarter of all the group's bombers were fitted with the new equipment and their crews trained as formation leaders, guiding 'gaggles' of other aircraft to the target area, all of which bombed on sight of the lead aircraft releasing its load. The first raid by No 3 Group in its new independent role, against Bonn on 18 October, was a complete success. From then on, daylight 'G-H' formation attacks, many in conditions of ten-tenths cloud, would become an important and regular feature of Bomber Command's offensive until the end of the war.

As the end of the year approached, most of Germany's major cities lay devastated. The Ruhr — much of it ruins — was being systematically cut off from the rest of Germany. Elsewhere, towns like Koblenz, Freiburg, Heilbronn and Ulm, which had hitherto remained untouched, were dealt crushing attacks, either as they found themselves cursed with strategic importance as the battlefront got nearer, or simply because more vital targets had already been destroyed. On 6/7 December, Harris extended Bomber Command's part in the oil campaign by despatching his first major attack on a synthetic oil plant in eastern Germany, in this case the huge complex at Leuna-Merseburg near Leipzig. However, despite their critical fuel situation, the Germans had been able to husband enough supplies for a surprise counter-offensive in the Ardennes, which got underway in mid-December. For the first crucial days, as Field Marshal von Rundstedt's *Panzers* attempted to drive a wedge between the British and American armies, poor flying weather precluded any response from the Allied air forces. When conditions finally improved, Bomber Command struck at enemy troop positions in Belgium, and stepped up its attacks on rail communications behind the battlefront to hamper the movement of German reinforcements. Lancasters equipped with 'G-H' played a vital role during these attacks, leading daylight strikes through solid undercasts. Over that final Christmas of the war, Harris's crews contributed much to the ultimate failure of Hitler's last gamble in the West.

Left:
Lancaster LL779/SR-V and its unidentified crew of No 101 Squadron at Ludford Magna, Lincolnshire, in February 1944. From October 1943, No 101 Squadron was equipped for a unique role in Bomber Command, that of radio countermeasures using equipment called 'Airborne Cigar' ('ABC'). As well as a normal bomb load, the squadron's Lancasters carried extra radio equipment and a German-speaking 'special operator', whose job was to tune into enemy air-to-ground R/T communications and jam them using a powerful transmitter. This aircraft was one of two from the squadron which failed to return from a costly operation to the synthetic oil plant at Homberg on 20/21 July 1944, when night-fighters claimed a total of 20 Lancasters. **HU 75739**

Right:
The King and Queen spent a day visiting three Pathfinder stations on 10 February 1944. Here they are seen talking to ground crew of No 156 Squadron at Warboys, Huntingdonshire, beneath the imposing bulk of one of the squadron's Lancasters protruding from a T2 hangar. No 156 was one of the original squadrons chosen to become the nucleus of the Pathfinder force in the summer of 1942. As an indication of the losses now being suffered by Bomber Command, the squadron lost 31 crews between January and the end of March — over half its total losses for 1944 in the first three months of the year. **CH 12153**

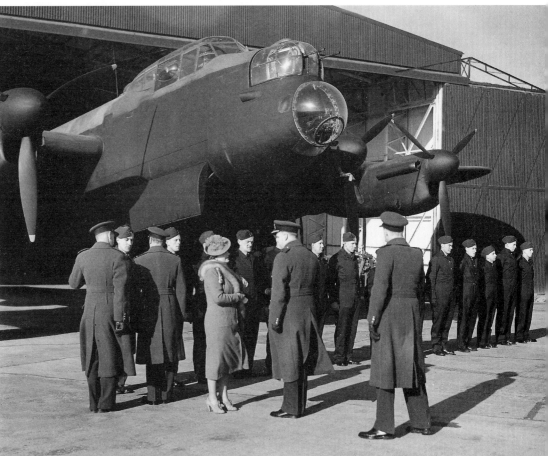

Above:
Flying Officer P. Ingleby from Manchester, a Lancaster navigator with No 619 Squadron, at work at his station, 14 February 1944. Facing him are the 'repeaters' of certain flight instruments — altimeter, airspeed indicator and compass — while above is the direction-finding receiver, and just visible on the right, the 'H2S' indicator and receiver; one of a host of aids available to the navigators of 1944. 'Gee' was still in use, and although its value over enemy territory had by this date been largely negated by jamming, it nevertheless provided a useful way of homing safely back to base. **CH 12288**

Right:
'Tail-end Charlie' — veteran air gunner Flight Lieutenant J. A. Howard DFC, at his position in the rear turret of the same Lancaster. The cramped, four-gun Fraser-Nash FN20 turret remained standard on Lancasters until the advent of the FN82 turret with twin .50in machine guns, which appeared on late production aircraft at the end of the war. Some units could not wait, however, and from June 1944 onwards, No 1 Group experimented with the privately-produced Rose-Rice turret, again equipped with twin .50in guns, as a way of increasing the Lancaster's defensive firepower. **CH 12282**

Left:
A WAAF airwoman belting-up .303in ammunition for the Lancasters of No 619 Squadron at Coningsby, February 1944. A Lancaster carried 10,000 rounds for its rear turret and 2,000 rounds apiece for the mid-upper and front turrets. Throughout the war the rifle calibre Browning machine gun remained the standard defensive armament in all RAF heavy bombers, resulting in the aircraft being outgunned and outranged by the heavier weapons of the German night-fighters. However, this mattered little in the war of stealth over Germany, when it was more important for the gunners to see their opponent in time, and call for evasive action, than to try and shoot it out. **CH 12285**

Left:
Don't forget Teddy! No 50 Squadron Lancaster skipper Flying Officer T. Blackham keeps a firm hold on the crew's lucky mascot, as he is helped into his flying jacket by his flight engineer, Sergeant C. Walton, at Skellingthorpe, 19 February 1944. Other members of the crew are, from left to right: Pilot Officer D. Jones (navigator), Sergeant H. Ridd (mid-upper gunner), Sergeant S. Smith (bomb aimer) and Sergeant S. Wilkins (wireless operator). That night, Bomber Command sent 823 aircraft to Leipzig and suffered catastrophic losses; 82 bombers were either shot down or crashed in Britain — the worst night of the war so far (but soon to be exceeded). This time No 50 Squadron was fortunate, and all got back. **CH 12209**

Above: A 4,000lb 'Cookie' is backed into position beneath a Lancaster II of No 408 (Goose) Squadron, RCAF, at Linton-on-Ouse, circa February 1944. The Lancaster II was powered by air-cooled Bristol Hercules radial engines, and was designed originally as an insurance against problems with the supply of Rolls-Royce Merlins. In the event, the feared shortages never materialised, and consequently only 300 aircraft were completed. The engines were found to be less prone to damage than the water-cooled Merlins, but offered poorer altitude performance. Most Lancaster IIs were fitted with bulged bomb doors, to accommodate an 8,000lb HC bomb, and ventral gun turrets. Six Bomber Command squadrons were equipped at various times with this variant, including three Canadian units in No 6 Group. No 408 converted back to Halifaxes in mid-1944, having flown 1,210 Lancaster sorties at a cost of 51 aircraft. **HU 56276**

Right:
The crew of Halifax III 'E-Edward' of No 51 Squadron at Snaith prepare to set off for Stuttgart on the evening of 1 March 1944. For the captain, Flight Lieutenant A. Caygill DFC (right), it would be his 28th trip. (Happily, he finished his tour of 30 'ops' a fortnight later when he returned safely from Frankfurt.) The fact that eight, and not the usual seven, crew members are in the photograph would perhaps indicate that a new pilot was being taken along as 'second dickey'. Though unpopular with established crews, it was routine for a new pilot on a squadron to fly a couple of operations with an experienced skipper before being let loose with his own aircraft and crew. **CH 12607**

Right:
The crew of Lancaster 'C-Charlie' of No 44 Squadron try to warm themselves in their Nissen hut quarters at Dunholme Lodge, after returning from Stuttgart, 2 March 1944. Accommodation at bomber bases could vary from substantial centrally-heated buildings at prewar Expansion Period aerodromes to draughty huts at the new satellite or dispersed locations. The Stuttgart raid came at a time when the main weight of Bomber Command's offensive was being directed against lesser German cities, following its failure to produce anything like the hoped-for German collapse during its prolonged assault on Berlin. On this occasion, thick cloud on the way to and from the target had kept the night-fighters out of the bomber stream, and only four aircraft were lost, including one from No 44 Squadron. **CH 12379**

Left:
A Stirling of No 149 Squadron at Lakenheath about to be loaded with a clutch of 1,500lb sea mines, March 1944. Bomber Command's mine-laying campaign was a great success; Harris claimed that almost 1,000 ships were sunk or damaged in the period between February 1942 and the end of the war, for an expenditure of approximately 1,100 mines per month. The shipment of iron ore from Spain and Sweden, the movement of supplies to Norway and the transport of military stores to the Eastern Front via the Baltic ports were all disrupted by Bomber Command's activities against the German mercantile fleet. The U-boat bases in western France and their training grounds in the Baltic were also targeted. Stirlings carried out their first 'Gardening' sorties in March 1942, and continued to carry out this important but unglamorous work until July 1944. No 149 Squadron flew a total of 160 mine-laying operations — the highest number in Bomber Command. **CH 12677**

Above: A Halifax III takes off from Elvington on 11 March 1944. In the background are aircraft of No 77 Squadron. Note the 'H2S' radar blister beneath the fuselage. This variant of the Halifax, which had begun to enter service in November 1943, was powered by Bristol Hercules air-cooled radial engines, which substantially improved performance when compared with the earlier Merlin-engined Halifax IIs and Vs. The Mk III was also the first to be equipped as standard with 'H2S' radar, although some aircraft were fitted instead with a ventral .50in gun position, owing to a shortage of sets. No 77 Squadron used Halifax IIIs operationally for the first time on 1/2 June 1944. **CH 12532**

The tension mounts in the crew room at Oakington on 18 March 1944 as Lancaster crews of No 7 Squadron wait to depart for Frankfurt. A game of cards helps pass the time for those able to concentrate. The raid was a successful one, inflicting considerable damage on the city. Thanks to a sizeable mine-laying operation near Heligoland, which lured away some of the night-fighters, losses were reasonably light (25 aircraft) and all No 7 Squadron crews returned. It was now becoming routine for a significant part of Bomber Command — in this case 200 aircraft — to be sent on diversionary sorties, which, though they sometimes split the German defences, also diluted the total effort which could be directed against the main target. **CH 12587**

Flight Sergeant Ed Clode of Invercargill, New Zealand, a bomb aimer with No 106 Squadron at Metheringham, has every reason to look pleased, having just returned from the Frankfurt raid of 22/23 March 1944, the last 'op' of his tour. Frankfurt suffered heavily on this and a previous raid by Bomber Command four nights earlier. To add to its misery, the American Eighth Air Force was over the city only 36hr later. The result was the complete destruction of the old city of Frankfurt, as well as a large number of industrial premises and official buildings. **CH 12540**

Above: A tense scene in the control tower at Snaith on the night of 30/31 March 1944 as personnel await the return of No 51 Squadron from Nuremberg. The duty Flying Control Officer communicates landing instructions to an approaching Halifax, while the Station Commander, Group Captain N. Fresson, keeps watch from the balcony outside. The disastrous Nuremberg operation, flown in bright moonlit conditions with little protective cloud, cost Bomber Command 105 aircraft, most of which were shot down in running battles with well-directed night-fighters. Strong winds blew many aircraft off course, so that a large number bombed Schweinfurt — some 50 miles from the target city — by mistake. For No 51 Squadron it was a particularly bad night; five aircraft failed to return, and another crashed near Oxford on its way back. A total of 35 aircrew were killed and seven captured. **CH 18743**

Right:
An armourer checks that the bomb doors are securely closed on a Mosquito IV of No 692 Squadron after a 4,000lb 'Cookie' has been squeezed aboard, at Graveley, Huntingdonshire, 4 April 1944. To carry such a load, the aircraft were modified with strengthened bomb bays and bulged bomb doors. No 692 Squadron was formed on 1 January 1944 and operated with No 8 (PFF) Group, forming part of the Light Night Striking Force (LNSF) which was so effective in carrying out diversionary and nuisance raids on German cities. The squadron became the first Mosquito unit to drop a 'Cookie' on Germany, during a raid on Düsseldorf on 23/24 February, and also dropped the first on Berlin, on 13/14 April 1944. **CH 12624**

Left:
The St Pierre-des-Corps railway marshalling yards at Tours, rendered virtually unusable after a visit by 180 Lancasters of No 5 Group on the night of 10/11 April 1944. On the same night, railway yards at Ghent, Laon, Aulnoye and Terginier were attacked by aircraft of other groups. By this date, Air Vice-Marshal Cochrane's No 5 Group had emerged as a semi-independent force, carrying out innovative low-level target-marking techniques using its own Mosquitos. As long as conditions were clear, these methods resulted in more accurate and concentrated bombing, which was vital during attacks on small targets in France and Belgium where civilian casualties had to be avoided if at all possible. **C 4332**

Above: The scene in the control room at East Kirkby, Lincolnshire, on the evening of 20 April 1944. Aircraft of No 57 Squadron, based at the station, were involved in an operation against the railway yards at La Chapelle, just north of Paris. Typically for this period, it was just one of several operations that night, with separate forces of bombers raiding Cologne as well as other French railway targets. In addition, there was the staple fare of Mosquito nuisance raids, radio countermeasures sorties, intruder missions and 'Gardening' operations, all designed to keep the German defences busy. From a total of 1,155 sorties flown, 15 aircraft were lost, including two Lancasters from No 57 Squadron. **CH 18718**

Above:
Sergeant W. Sinclair, RAF, and Flying Officer E. H. Giersch, RAAF, of No 463 Squadron at Waddington, test their oxygen masks in the crew room before an operational sortie, April 1944. Such checks were vital; a malfunctioning oxygen mask was enough to abort a sortie. No 463 Squadron had formed in November 1943 with Lancasters from 'C' Flight of No 467 Squadron, and was the last Australian unit to be raised in Bomber Command. **AUS 2000**

Left:
A line-up of Lancasters of No 514 Squadron at Waterbeach, circa April 1944. The squadron was formed at Foulsham, Norfolk, in September 1943, and originally equipped with the radial-engined Lancaster II. By this date, however, it was converting to Merlin-engined 'Lancs' as seen here. LM181/JI-E, in the middle of the photograph, was one of four aircraft lost by the squadron on the night of 20/21 July during a costly raid on the synthetic oil plant at Homberg in the Ruhr. There were no survivors from any of the crews. **CL 4214**

Left:
A Lancaster of No 300 (Masovian) Squadron receives attention at Faldingworth, Lincolnshire, on 25 April 1944. The somewhat rickety ladder providing access to the cockpit canopy would point to a lack of servicing equipment! The only Polish unit to operate Lancasters, No 300 Squadron moved to Faldingworth and re-equipped with the type in March 1944, after a long spell flying Wellingtons from the primitive grass airfield at Ingham. The Poles flew a total of 1,216 Lancaster sorties, losing 30 aircraft on operations. **HU 75016**

Left:
Sea mines wait to be loaded aboard a Halifax V Series IA of No 77 Squadron, probably at Full Sutton in Yorkshire, shortly after the airfield was opened in May 1944. The Halifax V was identical to the more common Mk II version, except for its simplified Dowty undercarriage, which replaced the more complex — and slower to produce — Messier units fitted to the Mk II. Both of these long-suffering early Halifax variants had been withdrawn from Main Force operations over Germany in February 1944 during the Battle of Berlin, but continued to fly 'Gardening' sorties and less hazardous trips to France, now a routine part of Bomber Command's diversionary operations. **CH 21145**

At an unidentified No 5 Group station in May 1944, Aircraftman W. Bush hands cans of film of target photographs to Corporal W. Teall, another member of the photographic section, who will deliver them by motorcycle combination to Group Headquarters for interpretation. Night flash photographs — taken automatically by a camera in the bomber — were vital in assessing bombing accuracy, but were hated by the crews because of the need to hold their aircraft straight and level for a further half-minute after the bombs had been dropped. A powerful 4.5in photoflash, which was released with the bombs, was used to illuminate the scene below. Because of manpower shortages, it was usual for station photographic sections to retrieve the film from returning bombers, develop and print it, and then deliver the results direct to Group Headquarters. **CH 13160**

Above: Armourers hitch a lift aboard bomb trains leaving the bomb dump at Snaith, June 1944. These are 500lb GP bombs of various types, some of the 395,000 that were dropped by Bomber Command in 1944 alone. A shortage of British-built bombs had to be made up by using American stocks. The use of 500-pounders had been declining in favour of larger, high-capacity bombs, but 'softening-up' attacks prior to the invasion of Europe, and the subsequent intensive bombing operations in support of the ground forces, necessitated a vast increase in their use. **CH 13407**

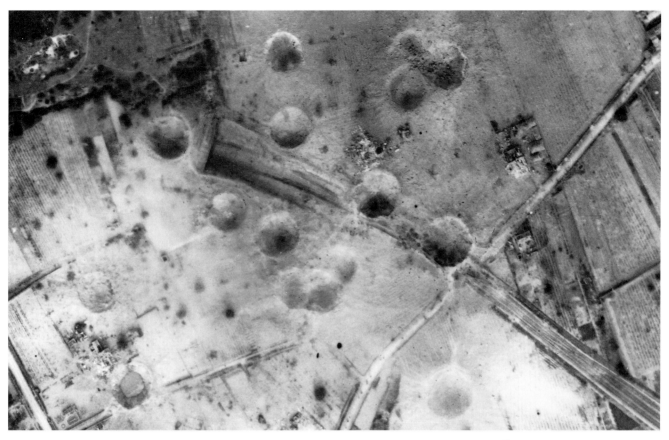

Above:
After the Dams raid of May 1943, No 617 Squadron retained its position in No 5 Group as a specialist precision bombing unit. Its skills were amply demonstrated on 8/9 June when the squadron dropped the first 12,000lb 'Tallboy' deep-penetration bombs — designed by Barnes Wallis — on a railway tunnel near Saumur, in order to block the passage of a German armoured division towards the Normandy battle area. This 'recce' photograph taken after the raid shows the mouth of the tunnel neatly bracketed by several near misses. As can be seen, one bomb scored a direct hit and penetrated the tunnel roof, blocking it completely, and two others demolished a section of the track. **CL 80**

Left:
The 'round the clock' bombing required during the period of D-Day and the campaign in Normandy necessitated close liaison between the Allied air forces. Even at squadron level, goodwill visits between neighbouring units fostered the spirit of co-operation, and made for good copy in the newspapers. Here B-17 Flying Fortress aircrew of the 96th Bomb Group, US Eighth Air Force, mingle with Lancaster crews of No 622 Squadron at Mildenhall in the spring of 1944. No 622 Squadron had been formed in August 1943 from 'C' Flight of No 15 Squadron, and both units continued operating from this Suffolk airfield. Note the unpainted 'Window' chute beneath the nose of the Lancaster. **PMI 19152**

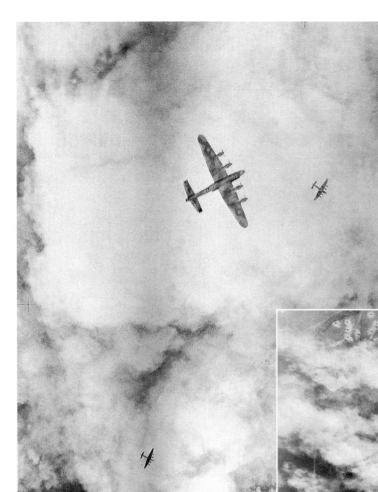

Left:
The summer of 1944 saw Bomber Command involved in its most intensive operations of the war so far. Supporting the Allied troops in Normandy and the renewal of raids against the German synthetic oil industry were the most vital tasks, but another call on its great strength was for attacks against V-1 flying bomb launching sites and stores, hidden in the countryside of the Pas de Calais. The V-1 campaign commenced on 16/17 June and continued until ground forces overran most of the sites in late August. In this dramatic view, Lancasters can be seen pounding one of three sites bombed on 2 July. Despite the cloud, bombing accuracy was good and no aircraft were lost. **C 4459**

Below:
On 6 July 1944 Bomber Command struck again at a 'large concrete structure' at Marquise Mimoyecques, midway between Calais and Boulogne. This underground site was the location of the as yet incomplete V-3 long-range gun, with which the Germans intended to bombard London. On this occasion No 617 Squadron employed the new 'Tallboy' deep-penetration bombs, one of which scored a direct hit on the concrete slab which covered the buried gun shafts. Halifaxes of No 4 Group were also involved, one of which is seen over the target in this photograph. After this raid there was no possibility of the site being completed, and it was soon overrun by the Allies. **C 4458**

Left:
The Duke of Gloucester, Governor-General Designate of the Commonwealth of Australia (standing fourth from right), watches armourers bombing-up Lancaster I LL964/AR-D2 of No 460 Squadron, RAAF, during his visit to Binbrook in July 1944. The Lancaster in the photograph was eventually lost when it crash-landed in Belgium during an operation to Cologne on 31 October/1 November 1944, while serving with No 103 Squadron. The circle on the forward fuselage was a gas detection patch, an archaic feature retained on No 1 Group aircraft. For some reason, the censor decided that the 'Window' chute on the underside of the nose of the aircraft should be obscured. **AUS 2017**

Above:

A job well done. Watched by the CO, Wing Commander D. A. Gardner (left), aircrew of No 166 Squadron at Kirmington, Lincolnshire, gather on 20 July 1944 to hear the Adjutant, Flight Lieutenant F. C. Tigh, read out a congratulatory message from Field Marshal Montgomery, thanking the bomber crews for their efforts supporting the British Second Army's armoured offensive in Normandy — Operation 'Goodwood'. On 18 July, Bomber Command had dropped over 5,000 tons of bombs in daylight attacks on various fortified villages in the line of the British tank advance east of Caen, severely disrupting the German defences. **CH 13551**

Right:

In the clothing store at an unidentified bomber station in August 1944, a WAAF section officer and her assistant issue new items of flying kit to two aircrew. The pilot officer in the foreground signs for an electrically-heated waistcoat and a pair of 1940 pattern boots, while, behind, another tries on an Irvin sheepskin flying jacket for size. The Women's Auxiliary Air Force had been formed in June 1939 to release men from certain ground trades for duties elsewhere. In 1944 nearly a quarter of all ground staff on RAF bomber bases were women. Although WAAF organisation and uniforms deliberately conformed closely to those of the RAF, rank titles were subtly different; for example, a section officer was the equivalent of a flying officer in the RAF. **CH 13713**

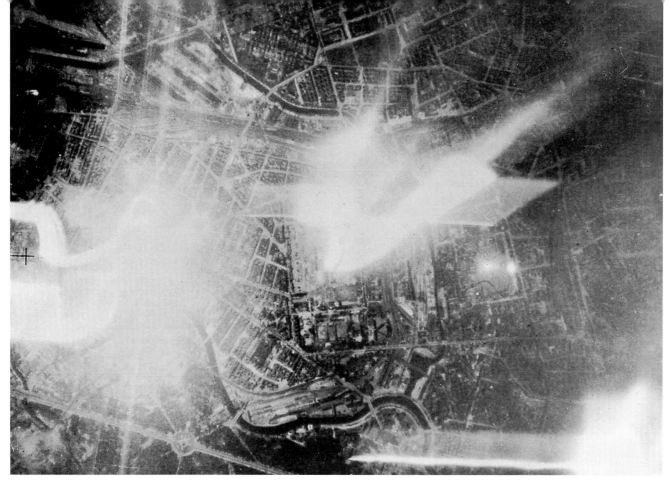

Above: On 11/12 August 1944, Mosquitos of the Light Night Striking Force were over Berlin for the second night in a row. This photograph over the centre of the city shows searchlight tracks and burning target indicators during the raid. The Charlottenburg Chausee can be seen running diagonally across the bottom of the photograph, through the Tiergarten district and on towards the Brandenburg Gate. The Reichstag is within the bend of the River Spree just above. The LNSF, which eventually grew to eight squadrons in No 8 (PFF) Group, was an undoubted success story. Between May 1943 and May 1945 it flew a total of 27,239 sorties, dropping 1,459 'Cookies' on Berlin alone, for the loss of a mere 196 aircraft. On this particular operation, one Mosquito was lost to flak. **C 4925**

Below: A Boeing Fortress III, HB796/G, equipped for radio countermeasures work, photographed in August 1944 at the Atlantic air terminal at Prestwick, where aircraft were modified for service in this role. No 214 Squadron operated Fortresses in the Norfolk-based No 100 Group from January 1944 onwards, first at Sculthorpe, until May, and then at Oulton, for the rest of the war. The squadron was involved in most types of radio and radar jamming work, so the equipment fit of the aircraft varied considerably. This particular Fortress has an 'H2S' radome under the nose, 'Airborne Grocer' airborne radar jamming aerials flanking the rear turret, and, on top of the fuselage, the transmission mast for the 'Airborne Cigar' ('ABC') equipment which drowned out German night-fighter control frequencies. Later, high-powered 'Jostle' jamming transmitters were carried instead of 'ABC', the Fortress being the only aircraft that could accommodate this equipment. **ATP 13090B**

Boys from the Luton Air Training Corps (ATC) were treated to a day at No 12 OTU at Chipping Warden, Northamptonshire, on 17 September 1944. The highlight for 15-year-old Cadet Tommy McMordie was the chance to try the rear turret of one of the unit's Wellingtons for size. The photographer noted that Tommy's ambition when he joined the RAF was to become a rear gunner. Fortunately, perhaps, the war would end long before he got the chance. A clear vision cut-out in the perspex had become standard in all bomber rear turrets by this date. **CH 13880**

Below:
Although the Belgian port of Antwerp had been occupied by the British Second Army on 4 September 1944, it could not be used while the mouth of the River Scheldt, on which it lay, was dominated by the German-held island of Walcheren. After a number of attacks on enemy artillery batteries there, Bomber Command despatched 252 Lancasters, led by seven 'Oboe' Mosquitos, on a daylight operation on 3 October to breach the island's protective dykes at Westkapelle. This reconnaissance photograph shows the result, a gap 75yd wide, through which the sea is flooding in. No aircraft were lost, but further attacks had to be carried out against the remaining dykes and gun batteries before the island was deemed ready for the seaborne assault, which took place on 1 November. **C 4668**

Above: A Lancaster destined for preservation after the war was W4783/AR-G of No 460 Squadron, RAAF, which was delivered in October 1942 and went on to complete 90 operations. 'G-George' flew its last 'op' on 20/21 April 1944; it was then retired and chosen for presentation to the Australian War Museum in Canberra, in recognition of the effort and sacrifice made by Australians in Bomber Command's offensive. With Flight Lieutenant E. A. Hudson DFC at the controls, the aircraft is seen running-up its engines at a rainswept Prestwick on 11 October, before setting out on its long journey. **AUS 2023**

Above: Two of the crew of 'G-George' prepare themselves for the flight to Australia in October 1944. In the foreground, Flying Officer C. H. Tindale DFM, wireless operator, warms up his set, while behind, the navigator, Flying Officer W. C. Gordon DFC, checks his equipment. Note the details of the T1154/R1155 transmitter/receiver, which was the standard radio set in use by Bomber Command. During its service with Bomber Command, 'G-George' was reputed to have been flown by 29 different pilots, and had 200 different men among its various crews. **AUS 2022**

Above: A famous image of a Halifax III of No 6 Group over the oil plant at Wanne-Eickel in the Ruhr on 12 October 1944. A directive issued to Bomber Command and the US Eighth Air Force on 25 September established the German petroleum industry as the primary objective for both forces and, despite Harris's objections to concentrating on what he termed 'panacea' targets, he directed a significant part of his Command's efforts to it. In the last quarter of 1944 Bomber Command carried out 27 heavy bomber attacks against 15 oil plants, dropping some 23,000 tons of bombs on them. Most raids were carried out in daylight with fighter cover, though by now the Luftwaffe was a spent force. Only one aircraft failed to return from this operation, but three more were written off in crashes in Britain on their return. **C 4713**

Above: A Halifax III of No 78 Squadron comes in to land at Breighton, after the first daylight raid on Essen, 25 October 1944. The shot was taken by a photographer working for the *Northern Echo* during an official visit. This major attack by 771 aircraft came after an even heavier raid two nights before. Both operations deluged the city with high explosives, crippling what industrial capacity remained after earlier assaults. Note the white horizontal bands on the aircraft's fins; in the latter half of 1944 most No 4 Group squadrons sported various distinctive tail markings to enable aircraft to assemble more easily during daylight operations. Bomber Command crews were not trained to fly tight formations like their American counterparts, but instead flew in loose 'gaggles'. Note too the duty pilot's control trailer in the foreground. **HU 83150**

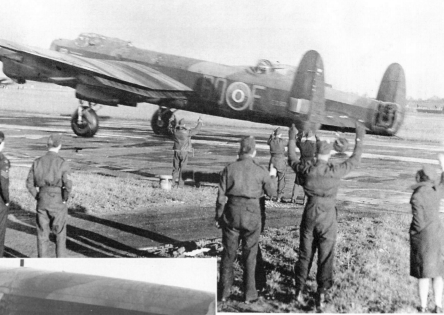

Right:
Lancaster III ED905/BQ-F of No 550 Squadron sets off from North Killingholme, Lincolnshire, on its 100th operation — to Düsseldorf — on the evening of 2 November 1944. A group of well-wishers gives the usual 'thumbs up' as it begins its take-off run. The pilot of 'F-Fox', Flight Lieutenant David Shaw, had been a sergeant in the Home Guard before joining the RAF in September 1942. In his words, he 'traded in a broomstick for a Lancaster'! Two other Lancasters of No 550 Squadron also completed over 100 operational sorties. **CH 14188**

Left:
Flying Officer J. Sanders DFC (third from right), and his cheerful crew of No 617 Squadron with their Lancaster, ME562/KC-K, following the successful daylight operation against the *Tirpitz* in Tromsö Fjord in Norway on 12 November 1944. In the third attempt to sink the battleship that autumn, a force of 30 specially adapted Lancasters from No 9 and No 617 Squadrons, operating from Lossiemouth in Scotland, once again attacked with 'Tallboy' bombs, two of which scored direct hits and capsized the vessel.
To save weight, the Lancasters had their dorsal turrets removed, and carried an extra 250 gallons of fuel in fuselage tanks for the very long 2,250-mile flight.
CH 17863

Right:
'Nick the Nazi Neutralizer', a veteran Lancaster III, LM130/JO-N, of No 463 Squadron, RAAF, is rearmed and refuelled at Waddington in early December 1944. By this date there were five Australian squadrons in Bomber Command, but none ever consisted wholly of RAAF aircrew. On 11 March 1945 this Lancaster collided with a Hurricane near Sleaford in Lincolnshire during fighter affiliation training. Pilot Officer Orchard, RAAF, and his English crew were all killed. **UK 2417**

Above: Halifax III MZ817/DT-Q of No 192 Squadron, and flown by Flying Officer N. Irvine, which crashed on take-off at Foulsham on the evening of 9 December 1944. This squadron was a specialist unit formed in January 1943 for radio countermeasures and electronic intelligence work, operating in No 3 Group until December 1943 when it joined the newly formed No 100 (Bomber Support) Group. Although the squadron also operated Wellingtons and Mosquitos, the Halifax III was the chosen heavy aircraft for this sort of work; its fuselage was capacious enough to accommodate any number of 'black boxes' and also carry a bomb load for use against Main Force targets. From October 1944 the unit began operations with the Special 'Window' Force, taking part in the various diversionary and 'spoof' raids intended to confuse the enemy further and waste his precious stocks of aviation fuel. **HU 60601**

Above: A Lancaster over the railway yards at Rheydt, near Mönchengladbach, on 27 December 1944, one of the many transport targets behind the Ardennes battle area attacked by Bomber Command over the New Year period. A force of 200 Lancasters and 11 Mosquitos was involved in this operation. Two aircraft were lost, one of which, a Lancaster of No 75 Squadron, was struck by a bomb from another aircraft above. This was by no means a rare occurrence, and was a hazard faced by crews even in daylight. **C 4875**

1945

'In the last year of the war Bomber Command played a major part in the almost complete destruction of whole vital segments of German oil production, in the virtual dislocation of her communications system and in the elimination of other important activities.'

(Official History, HMSO, 1961)

As 1945 dawned, Allied strategy was not proceeding quite as planned. Bomber Command, along with the American and tactical air forces, was heavily engaged in containing the German counter-offensive in the Ardennes, a battle which had diverted British and American troops and delayed plans for commencing the final advance into Germany itself. Among the Allied leaders, there was more than a little frustration that the long-awaited German capitulation had still not occurred, despite the increasingly desperate straits in which the Third Reich now found itself. In the East, huge Soviet armies were about to begin their final headlong advance, so that by the end of January their tanks would be on German soil. Pressed from all sides, with its aerial defences shattered and capable of offering only token resistance, Germany lay exposed to the climax of the strategic bomber offensive, in which Bomber Command's still-expanding strength would, in those last four months of the war, contribute a vast 185,000 tons of bombs and sea mines; a total greater than had been expended between September 1939 and the middle of 1943!

Sir Arthur Harris now controlled a force with an available strength of over 1,400 aircraft, the vast majority Lancasters, which equipped no fewer than 51 squadrons. Another six squadrons would be created before the end of the war, so that by April his Command would reach its wartime peak of 1,625 bombers. Thanks to the almost total Allied air superiority, losses were at an all-time low, but the German defences would continue to claim victims until the very end. Flak, accidents and desperate rearguard actions by the last of the Luftwaffe would result in more than 800 aircraft failing to return, or being written off, while on operations during the last three effective months of the bomber offensive. The pattern of operations set in the final quarter of 1944 would continue into the new year, with Bomber Command's main effort divided between attacks on industrial cities, oil and transport targets. By now, the effects on individual target systems were merging and becoming increasingly difficult to separate. Area attacks on industrial cities, especially in the Ruhr, were having an important secondary effect by wrecking some of the smaller oil targets and disrupting communications and power supplies; at the same time, specific attacks on the enemy's transport infrastructure were contributing massively to the breakdown of German industry, by preventing the flow of coal, raw materials and components.

Above: Flight Sergeant George Thompson, a wireless operator with No 9 Squadron, was posthumously awarded the Victoria Cross for his gallantry on 1 January 1945 during a raid on the Dortmund-Ems Canal near Ladbergen. In a daylight operation, a force of 102 Lancasters and two Mosquitos of No 5 Group successfully breached a section of the newly-repaired canal, with the loss of only two aircraft. One of these, a Lancaster piloted by Flying Officer R. Denton, was hit by an 88mm flak shell shortly after completing its bomb run and set on fire. Flight Sergeant Thompson rescued both gunners from their turrets, sustaining terrible burns himself in the process. The Lancaster made a successful crash-landing in Allied territory, but Thompson and one of the gunners later succumbed to their injuries. In this record portrait, Flight Sergeant Thompson wears the 'signaller' brevet introduced in December 1943 for specialist wireless operators, which replaced the old 'AG' brevet. **CH 14685**

Operations were also carried out against naval objectives and in direct support of the ground offensive. The American contribution followed similar lines, and, as the end of the war approached, the combined bomber forces finally fell into step, relentlessly pounding Germany by night and day in a concerted effort of immense proportions.

The year began with some dramatic precision attacks: Mosquitos of No 8 Group successfully lobbed 4,000lb 'Cookies' into the mouths of tunnels in the Eifel region, through which ran vital reinforcement routes between Germany and the Ardennes sector, and Lancasters of No 5 Group once again punctured the banks of the Dortmund-Ems and Mittelland canals. The Main Force squadrons carried out major area raids on Nuremberg, Munich and Stuttgart, but it was the continuation of attacks on the German petroleum industry and communications that now dominated operations. During January and February, Bomber Command dropped a greater tonnage of bombs on oil targets than did the USAAF, and was proving to be more accurate and destructive in the poor weather than the Americans. On 13/14 January, 218 Lancasters and seven Mosquitos of No 5 Group reduced the major oil plant at Pölitz, near Stettin, to ruins. A second raid on 8/9 February effectively finished it off; not even the Germans' famed ability to repair damage and restore production could cope with this level of destruction. Major attacks were also directed against the synthetic oil installations at Zeitz and Leuna, and smaller, equally effective raids were carried out against the remaining fuel storage depots and benzol plants scattered throughout Germany. By March, all the major oil targets — and many of the smaller ones — had been destroyed, and the German armed forces virtually paralysed.

Bomber Command's contribution to the campaign against enemy communications was just as successful, and was having similarly profound effects on German industrial production in the final months of the war. Operations ranged from precision strikes against viaducts and bridges by Nos 9 and 617 Squadrons to major Main Force raids on railway centres, but it was No 3 Group, operating independently, and thanks to 'G-H' able to bomb through thick cloud, that undertook the majority of attacks on marshalling yards. The so-called 'Ruhr Plan' was intended to dislocate the main rail and canal routes leading out of the Ruhr, and thus interfere decisively with the transport of coal and industrial supplies. The vital choke-points were well known; on 21/22 February the Mittelland Canal section near Gravenhorst was again breached and drained for the last time. At the beginning of March, the Ladbergen aqueduct on the Dortmund-Ems Canal was also put out of action. The Bielefeld railway viaduct, which connected the Ruhr with northern Germany, resisted all attempts by No 5 Group to sever it with 'Tallboys' during February, but was finally brought down by a 22,000lb 'Grand Slam' 'earthquake' bomb on 14 March. In the days that followed, other key viaducts and bridges were demolished using combinations of these mighty weapons.

In February, Bomber Command was directed by political order to undertake a more controversial operation. In their mood of frustration during early January, the Allied planners had seen fit to dust off plans for Operation 'Thunderclap', originally conceived in the summer of 1944. 'Thunderclap' aimed to administer a pulverising blow by Anglo-American bomber forces against key German cities at a critical moment when the enemy's military situation seemed irretrievable, in order to produce such confusion and chaos that an immediate surrender would occur. It was now decided that a series of devastating area raids on major communication centres immediately behind the Eastern Front, packed with refugees and wounded troops fleeing from the Russians, would cause massive transport and administrative chaos, thus facilitating the Russian advance and hopefully shortening the war. Churchill, under pressure from Stalin, was keen to use the Allied heavy bomber

force in this way, despite opposition from his own ministers and service chiefs, and instructed the Air Staff to plan an attack. Berlin, Chemnitz, Dresden and Leipzig, all vital nodal points and supply routes behind the German lines, were selected as suitable targets.

On 27 January, Sir Arthur Harris received orders to prepare Bomber Command's involvement in 'Thunderclap'. The plan was continually delayed by the weather, but began on 3 February with a raid by the USAAF on Berlin. After a further period of waiting, Bomber Command then went to Dresden on the night of 13/14 February, delivering a typically accurate and concentrated attack in two distinct and separate waves, the second of which produced a firestorm not seen since Hamburg in July 1943. Somewhere in the region of 50,000 people were consumed; six RAF aircraft were lost. On the next night Chemnitz was attacked, but with much less effect as a result of a layer of cloud obscuring the target. Other cities in western Germany suffered their own ordeals as Bomber Command carried out further night area raids. Duisburg was hit hard, for the last time, on 21/22 February, and Mainz weathered its last

Below: The Gravenhorst section of the Mittelland Canal, where it crosses the River Aa, after an attack by No 5 Group on the night of 1/2 January 1945, which successfully breached the banks of the waterway. The concentration of bomb craters shows up clearly against the snow-covered landscape. The Mittelland and Dortmund-Ems Canals were two of the key communications targets chosen for priority attacks in order to isolate the Ruhr from the rest of Germany. The sections of these two waterways considered most vulnerable, at Gravenhorst and Ladbergen respectively, had been hit — and repaired — many times before, and would be targeted again before hostilities ended. As a result of the raids, canal traffic, much of it coal, was reduced to a fraction of that normally carried. **C 4897**

Above: This crashed Halifax III at a frozen Full Sutton in early January 1945 was the centrepiece of a posed sequence illustrating the work of WAAF nursing orderlies. Corporal Dennett and Aircraftwoman Agnes Hall, both aged 23, attend to an 'injured' crew member as other ground personnel pose awkwardly by the pilot's escape hatch. For much of the war 'aerodrome duty' had been the sole preserve of male medical personnel, since dealing with grievously wounded aircrew was considered unsuitable work for women. However, a shortage of medical orderlies eventually forced the Air Ministry to amend its rules and accept women volunteers. The Halifax is MZ335/KN-A of No 77 Squadron, which suffered an engine failure when taking-off for Ludwigshafen on the afternoon of 2 January, and bellied-in beyond the airfield perimeter. The crew escaped unhurt but the aircraft was declared a write-off. **CH 14526**

and most damaging raid of the war at the end of the month. Pforzheim, a new target for the bombers, was visited by 367 Lancasters on 23/24 February, and suffered the third highest death toll of any German city after Dresden and Hamburg, when over 17,000 people were killed. The Master Bomber on this raid, Captain Edwin Swales of the South African Air Force, flying with No 582 Squadron, won the last Bomber Command VC of the war — posthumously — when his aircraft was hit by a night-fighter over the target. Despite severe damage to his aircraft, Swales continued to direct the raid and then kept the Lancaster in the air long enough for his crew to escape, but was unable to do so himself.

In March, Bomber Command flew practically 'round the clock', and delivered an unsurpassed weight of bombs. Essen, that most sacred of all objectives, was raided by over 1,000 aircraft during its ultimate attack on 11 March. The next day a similar force dropped a record 4,851 tons of explosives on Dortmund, effectively bringing to a halt any remaining industrial production there. Chemnitz was struck again as part of the continuing Operation 'Thunderclap', and final raids were carried out against Mannheim, Cologne and Nuremberg. During the last of these, on 16/17 March, night-fighters infiltrated the stream and exacted a heavy retribution, shooting down 24 Lancasters — almost 9% of the force. The shipyards in Hamburg attracted attacks aimed at disrupting production of potent new U-boat designs which had been worrying the Admiralty. Another U-boat target was the enormous concrete shelter at Farge, at the mouth of the Weser near Bremen, at that time the largest concrete structure in the world. Despite its 23ft thick roof, it was neatly perforated and knocked out by No 617 Squadron on 27 March, using 'Grand Slams'. All these attacks were interspersed with a host of further operations against railway yards and bridges, the few oil plants still functioning, and defended towns in the path of the Allied advance. Bomber Command's offensive had risen to a crescendo.

By the end of March, Allied troops were across the Rhine and advancing deep into Germany; in early April, the Ruhr was encircled. There now remained few strategic targets worthy of

attention from the vast armada of bombers available. The German capital continued to be raided by Mosquitos of the LNSF. Other cities were also attacked, but from late February onwards few nights went by when Berliners were not forced to the shelters by the presence of these aircraft over their city. On 14/15 April, Potsdam, on the outskirts of Berlin, was attacked by 512 'heavies', the last sizeable Bomber Command raid on a German city. By this time, much of Germany had been overrun and strategic operations had been wound down, the objective now being to facilitate the capture of the northern German ports. The island of Heligoland, guarding the approach to Hamburg, was pummelled by almost 1,000 aircraft on 18 April; a week later, coastal batteries on the Frisian island of Wangerooge, which dominated the approaches to Bremen and Wilhelmshaven, were dealt a similar blow. The last raid by the RAF's heavy bombers was despatched against an oil refinery at Tonsberg in southern Norway on 25/26 April. Thereafter, the Lancasters began flying humanitarian missions to bring back newly liberated prisoners of war, and drop food supplies to the starving Dutch, cut off in the enemy-occupied Netherlands. To the Mosquitos of No 8 Group fell the distinction of carrying out the very last offensive operation by Bomber Command, against shipping at Kiel on the night of 2/3 May. Sadly, losses were suffered right to the very end; one Mosquito and two Halifax radio countermeasures aircraft, all from No 100 Group which was supporting the raid, failed to return. They were the very last casualties in Bomber Command's long war, which was now over.

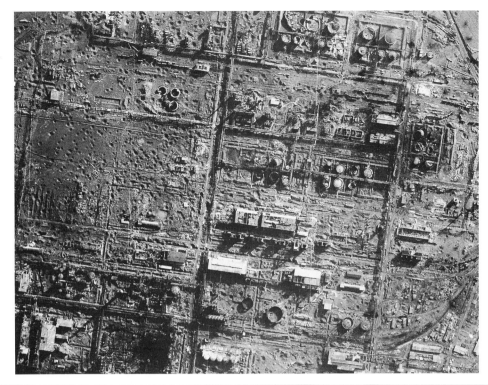

Left:

The Braunkohle-Benzin synthetic oil plant at Zeitz near Leipzig which was attacked on 16/17 January 1945, one of four oil targets chosen for that night's operations. The plant, one of the largest in Germany, had undergone several attacks by the USAAF during the summer of 1944. It had always managed to effect sufficient repairs to resume production, but the Bomber Command raid in January caused so much damage that the plant was effectively abandoned, as revealed in this reconnaissance photograph taken a month after the raid. **C 4985**

Below:

A photo-reconnaissance Mosquito IX, ML897 'D-Dorothy', of No 1409 (Meteorological) Flight, with air and ground crew and the Station Commander, Group Captain E. Donaldson (centre), at Wyton in January 1945. The 'Met' Flight was formed at Oakington in April 1943 under No 8 (PFF) Group control, and carried out weather reconnaissance flights in advance of Bomber Command and US Eighth Air Force raids until the end of the war. A total of 1,364 sorties were flown, including 161 by this aircraft alone. In that time only three Mosquitos were lost. **CH 14466**

Left:
Mechanics toil over the port-outer Merlin of a No 75 (New Zealand) Squadron Lancaster at Mepal, Cambridgeshire, on 9 February 1945. Delivered to the squadron in July 1944, HK593/JN-X had since become a veteran of 40 operations, with its gunners claiming one enemy aircraft destroyed. That night the squadron sent 21 aircraft in a No 3 Group attack on the Hohenbudberg railway yards at Krefeld, while other groups raided the oil plants at Pölitz and Wanne-Eickel. No 75 Squadron remained the only New Zealand night bomber unit in Bomber Command, and would end the war having flown more sorties than any other squadron. Unfortunately it also suffered the second highest casualty rate, losing 193 aircraft in action. **CH 14681**

Above:
The German fortress town of Kleve, photographed from a low-flying Auster aircraft, a few days after the major Bomber Command raid on 7/8 February 1945 carried out as a prelude to Operation 'Veritable', the British and Canadian advance into Germany west of the Rhine. On the same night, a large force of bombers also attacked Goch, another key objective, which formed part of the German defences south of the Reichswald. Both towns were heavily damaged, with Kleve virtually reduced to rubble. In the event, the blocked streets in the ruined town actually hindered the British advance. **C4964**

Left:
Where do old Wellingtons go? This one ended up mounted on bricks at an RAF rehabilitation centre at Loughborough, one of three such establishments in the country for the treatment of aircrew and ground staff recovering from major injuries. Supervised by a warrant officer member of staff (left), two bomber pilots are seen climbing into the Wellington in early March 1945. Sessions in the aircraft formed part of a wide-ranging programme of activities which were intended not only to restore the physical abilities of injured airmen, but also to help them deal with the mental and emotional problems associated with major trauma. As well as traditional exercises and physiotherapy, familiarisation sessions with cockpit, radio and navigation equipment were available; even workshops for ground personnel to relearn their trades. The centres claimed a success rate of over 80% of aircrew orthopaedic cases being classified as fit for flying duties at the end of their treatment. **CH 14977**

Left:

Crew members of Lancaster PA995/BQ-V of No 550 Squadron board their aircraft at North Killingholme for its 100th operation on 5 March 1945. Left to right are: Sergeant J. Nicholson (mid-upper gunner), Flight Sergeant Jack Bold (bomb aimer) and Sergeant M. McCutcheon (rear gunner). That night, Bomber Command's main effort was directed at Chemnitz, in a continuation of Operation 'Thunderclap'. An additional, smaller force went to the synthetic oil refinery at nearby Böhlen. The skipper, Flying Officer G. Blackler, brought 'V-Victor' home safely, and successfully completed his own operational tour. Two nights later, on its very next trip, and with a fresh crew aboard, 'V-Victor' was shot down — one of 18 Lancasters lost on an operation to Dessau. **CH 14855**

Below:

Halifaxes under cover in No 2 Hangar at Dishforth in March 1945. Dishforth was one of four operational training stations serving the Canadian squadrons of No 6 Group, and was home to No 1664 Heavy Conversion Unit, operating various marks of Halifax. In the autumn of 1944 the Canadian training units came under the administrative control of the RAF as No 76 Base, but retained their close links with the operational Canadian squadrons. Note the Airspeed Oxford, wearing the unit codes 'DH', tucked away in a corner of the hangar. **HU 56271**

Above:
Aircrew of No 347 (Tunisie) Squadron, French Air Force, with one of their Halifaxes at Elvington, March 1945. Although flying equipment is standard RAF issue, their uniforms and insignia distinguish them from their British and Commonwealth counterparts. No 347 Squadron was the second of the two French heavy bomber units to serve in Bomber Command, and formed in June 1944, a month after No 346 (Guyenne) Squadron. Many of the original aircrew had previously served with the French Air Force in North Africa before coming to Britain. Both units operated from Elvington as part of No 4 Group. **OWIL 51916**

Right:
Pour Hitler — the intended recipient and the cross of Lorraine are chalked on this 2,000lb HC bomb being winched into one of the French Halifaxes at Elvington. Note the three arming pistols on the end face of the 'Cookie'. The two French squadrons operated Halifax IIIs, but in March 1945 began to take delivery of the new Mk VI version with its more powerful engines. They flew over 2,700 sorties before the end of the war, losing 30 aircraft. **OWIL 51912**

Left:
'Clapper Kite' — Lancaster I (Special) PD119/YZ-J of No 617 Squadron, one of 33 aircraft modified in February 1945 to carry the 22,000lb 'Grand Slam' deep-penetration bomb, Bomber Command's most awesome weapon. In order to reduce weight as much as possible, the Mk I Specials flew without wireless operators, and had their front and mid-upper turrets removed, with the result that, once rid of their 10-ton loads, they 'went like the clappers'. The first operational drop of a 'Grand Slam' was made on 14 March, when 14 Lancasters carrying 'Tallboys' and one with a 'Grand Slam' destroyed the Bielefeld railway viaduct which carried the main line from Hamm to Hannover. Note the 'day' camouflage scheme, the squadron codes painted on the tailplane surfaces, and the marking outlining the dinghy stowage in the starboard wing root. **MH 30794**

Right:
A Lancaster, believed to be of No 300 (Masovian) Squadron, over the Deutsche Vacuum oil refinery at Bremen; it was one of 133 bombers involved in this daylight raid on 21 March 1945. As was now commonplace, Luftwaffe opposition was absent. Flak, too, was light and no losses were suffered. March 1945 found Bomber Command at the zenith of its power, dropping a greater tonnage of bombs in that month — 67,637 tons — than in the whole of the first two years and 10 months of the war. **C 5101**

Right:
'Able Mabel', otherwise known as Lancaster III ND458/HW-A of No 100 Squadron, had completed 121 operational sorties when this photograph was taken on 2 April 1945 at Waltham, Lincolnshire. Her skipper, Flight Lieutenant J. D. Playford, RCAF, shakes hands with Sergeant W. Hearn, flanked by other members of the aircraft's regular ground crew. They are LAC J. Cowls and Corporal R. Withey, on the left, with LAC J. Robinson and AC J. Hale, on the right. Another three 'Lancs' in No 100 Squadron passed the 100-operations mark. 'Mabel' ended the war with 123 trips and two enemy aircraft to her credit. **CH 14986**

Above: A scene of complete devastation in the railway yards at Münster, as discovered by British ground forces on 7 April 1945. The administrative centre of Westphalia, and a major rail junction, Münster had suffered heavy Bomber Command and USAAF attacks when it became a tactically important reinforcement route into the Rhine battle area. The last Bomber Command attack came on 25 March, by which time a total of 3,800 tons of bombs had been dropped on the town. Note the locomotive in the background, flung into the air by the force of a huge explosion. As well as directly hindering the movement of her armies, the bombing campaign against Germany's transport infrastructure was of vital importance in undermining industrial production during the last months of the war. **CL 2370**

Above:
Bomber Command's long campaign against Germany's capital ships continued almost to the very end of the war. On 9/10 April a strong force of Lancasters attacked the harbour area of Kiel. The heavy cruiser *Admiral Scheer*, which had recently fled from Gdynia in Poland to escape the Russian advance, was hit and capsized in one of the dockyard basins. She is seen here on 5 May with the ruins of Kiel in the background. The *Admiral Hipper* and *Emden* were also badly damaged, as was the Deutsche Werke U-boat yard. A week after the *Admiral Scheer* was capsized, the *Lützow* was sunk at her moorings at Swinemünde on the Baltic by No 617 Squadron. **CL 2772**

Above: One of the most symbolic of all Bomber Command's targets was Hitler's mountain retreat at Berchtesgaden in the Bavarian Alps, which was attacked on 25 April 1945. A force of 359 Lancasters and 16 Mosquitos bombed Hitler's chalet, the Berghof, and the nearby SS barracks, inflicting considerable damage despite problems finding and marking the target. In this photograph a Lancaster is seen over the target, which is already shrouded in smoke and fires. Two aircraft were lost. **C 5247**

Above:
A bomb-shattered residential district in Hamburg, photographed from an Auster communications aircraft on 3 May 1945, the day the city officially surrendered to the British. The last Bomber Command raid on Hamburg occurred on the night of 13/14 April with an attack by 87 Mosquitos of the LNSF. By then there was little left to bomb. As he scribbled his notes in the aircraft, the photographer was moved to remark that 'almost the whole city is in ruins'. Such scenes were repeated throughout Germany, the extent of the damage only becoming truly apparent from the air at low-level. **CL3400**

Left:
Operation 'Manna'. Between 29 April and 7 May 1945, Lancasters of Bomber Command dropped food supplies to the starving Dutch in those parts of Holland still occupied by the Germans, who had declared a local truce. Over 3,000 sorties were flown, delivering 6,672 tons of food. (The USAAF also took part, naming their effort Operation 'Chowhound'.) Here, ground crew of No 514 Squadron at Waterbeach struggle to load cement bags full of foodstuffs into the space where incendiaries and high explosives were once carried, 29 April 1945. **CL 2490**

Above:

Operation 'Exodus'. With the end of the war only days away, Bomber Command began its part in the huge task of ferrying newly-released prisoners of war back to Britain. Operations to Brussels and other airfields began on 26 April and continued until 1 June. This photograph was taken on 6 May 1945 at Juvincourt airfield near Rheims. Australian, New Zealand and British POWs wait to board a Lancaster of No 463 Squadron, RAAF, which bears the usual 'Aussie' graffiti. Some 500 POWs per day were repatriated from this airfield alone. By 1 June, approximately 75,000 men had been brought home by Bomber Command. **HU 74919**

Right:

Operation 'Exodus'. The war is over and Lancasters of No 635 Squadron prepare to taxi out at Lübeck on 11 May 1945 with more ex-POWs destined for repatriation. Each Lancaster could carry 24 men in addition to a skeleton crew. These Lancasters were some of the handful fitted at the end of the war with AGLT radar-directed rear gun turrets, codenamed 'Village Inn', in which the guns were automatically sighted and fired at enemy aircraft. However, they arrived too late to prove themselves in action. The Meteor jet fighters visible in the background are also worthy of note. **BU 5889**

BIBLIOGRAPHY

Blanchett, Chris, *From Hell, Hull and Halifax: an Illustrated History of No 4 Group 1937-1948* (Midland Counties Publications, 1992)

Bowyer, Chaz, *Mosquito at War* (Ian Allan, 1973)
Pathfinders at War (Ian Allan, 1977)

Bowyer, Michael J. F., *2 Group RAF: A Complete History, 1936-1945* (Faber & Faber, 1974)

Chorley, W. R., *RAF Bomber Command Losses of the Second World War, Vols 1-6* (Midland Counties Publications, 1992-1998)

Delve, Ken, *The Source Book of the RAF* (Airlife Publishing, 1994)

Falconer, J., *The Bomber Command Handbook 1939-1945* (Sutton Publishing, 1998)

Franks, Norman, *Valiant Wings: The Battle and Blenheim Squadrons over France 1940* (Crécy Books, 1994)

Garbett, Mike, & Goulding, Brian, *The Lancaster at War* (Ian Allan, 1971)

Gomersall, Bryce, *The Stirling File* (Air-Britain and Aviation Archæologist Publications, 1979)

Goulding, James, & Moyes, Philip, *RAF Bomber Command and its Aircraft 1936-1940* (Ian Allan, 1975)

Harris, Marshal of the RAF Sir Arthur, *Bomber Offensive* (Collins, 1947)

Hastings, Max, *Bomber Command* (Michael Joseph, 1979)

Mason, Francis K., *The Avro Lancaster* (Aston Publications, 1989)
The British Bomber since 1914 (Putnam, 1994)

Maynard, John, *Bennett and the Pathfinders* (Arms & Armour, 1996)

Merrick, K. A., *The Handley Page Halifax* (Aston Publications, 1990)

Middlebrook, Martin, & Everitt, Chris, *The Bomber Command War Diaries* (revised edition) (Midland Publishing, 1996)

Middlebrook, Martin, *The Nuremberg Raid* (Penguin, 1986)
The Peenemünde Raid (Penguin, 1988)
The Battle of Hamburg (Allen Lane, 1982)

Moyes, Philip J. R., *Bomber Squadrons of the RAF and their Aircraft* (Macdonald, 1964)

Roberts, R. N., *The Halifax File* (Air-Britain and Aviation Archæologist Publications, 1982)

Streetly, Martin, *The Aircraft of 100 Group* (Robert Hale, 1984)

Sweetman, John, *The Dambusters Raid* (Arms & Armour, 1990)

Terraine, John, *The Right of the Line* (Hodder & Stoughton, 1985)

Webster, Sir Charles, and Frankland, Noble, *The Strategic Air Offensive against Germany, 1939-1945* (HMSO, 1961)